High-rise and the Sustainable City

edited by
Han Meyer and
Daan Zandbelt

High Rise and the Sustainable City
Edited by Han Meyer and Daan Zandbelt
2012, Amsterdam 192 pages
ISBN: 978-90-8594-049-4

Keywords: Urban form, Density, sLIM, High-Rise, Skyline, Skyscrapers,
Quality of life, Sustainability

Text Editing: Dianna Beaufort
Lay-Out and Design: Ingeborg Scheffers
Cover Illustration: Daan Zandbelt and Ingeborg Scheffers

Published and distributed by Techne Press, Amsterdam, The Netherlands
www.technepress.nl

This publication has been financially supported by the Dutch Council
on Tall Buildings (Stichting Hoogbouw) Rotterdam, The Netherlands
and the Faculty of Architecture, Delft University of Technology, The Netherlands

This publication is based on the sLIM course no. 15, Spring 2010
High-Rise in the Sustainable City, to which all authors contributed with a lecture.
The foundation sLIM stimulates the knowledge of intensive and multiple use of space.

High-rise and the
Sustainable City

Table of Contents

Introduction - High-rise and
the Sustainable City

Han Meyer 8

1

High-rise Buildings and
Sustainable Urban Form

Peter Bosselmann 16

2

High-rise – Genesis and
Exodus of a Type

Markus Appenzeller 30

3

European Approaches to Managing
Higher Densities and Higher
Buildings: London's Ascendancy

Lora Nicolaou 44

4

Citius, Altius, Fortius:
Myths about High-rise

Daan Zandbelt 66

5

Sustainable Urban Form

Meta Berghauser Pont 78

6

High-rise and Rotterdam

Emiel Arends 94

7

Planning and Visibility Assessment of High
Building Development in The Hague

Frank van der Hoeven and Steffen Nijhuis 102

8

High-rise Buildings : A Contribution to
Sustainable Construction in the City?

Andy van den Dobbelsteen 120

9

Sustainable High-rise in Dutch Cities

Kees Kaan 148

10

The Eco Skyscraper : Designing
Sustainable Intensive Buildings

Robert Powell 166

About the Authors 188

Introduction

High-rise and the Sustainable City

Han Meyer

High-rise buildings and cities have had a long relationship with each other – but not a self-evident one. Throughout history, the reasons for building high-rises have changed, though some have stayed the same. Until the 20th century, the most important reason for constructing tall buildings in the city was to express power and wealth, as well as providing military strength. The famous towers of Italian towns like San Gimignano and Bologna are examples of this combination of a representation of the power and wealth of a family with the practical purpose of building military bastions for times of conflict. The first high-rise buildings in New York and Chicago did not have this military function anymore, but still their most important function was to impress, to be dominant in the city's the image. As Thomas van Leeuwen shows in his wonderful book *The Skyward Trend of Thought*, this first generation of high-rise buildings had nothing to do with a lack of land or with attempts to reduce land costs. They were built in vacant parts of the city, where land prices were low. Later on, they attracted new high-rise initiatives in the same area, with the after effect that land prices went up. So it was the other way round: high-rise was not a result of, but a reason for raising land prices.

Yet still this motive of building to impress is fully alive. The competition among cities like Kuala Lumpur, Dubai or Seoul to build the highest tower in the world is a continuation of this tradition.

Since the 20th century, other arguments for building high-rises have evolved. The idea that high-rise could be an instrument of urban land-use reorganization, and could even be the crucial element for creating the Ideal City, is typical of the 20th century. Le Corbusier, and with him many others of the Modern Movement, pleaded for the "vertical city" as an alternative to the *rue corridor* (corridor street) and the *île fermé* (perimeter block). A modern urban landscape of high-rise towers in a park-like environment would liberate people from the stress of noise and pollution in the traditional city and would create better living conditions for mankind and a better society. However, many projects built on Le Corbusier's principles ended up the opposite: they became the city's lost spaces, territories of social despair and decay, and sometimes demolished after only a few decades.

Jane Jacobs' famous book *The Death and Life of Great American Cities* was a sharp indictment against the "modernization" of American cities that resulted in a transformation of lively urban neighborhoods into desolate deserts of expressways and high-rise blocks. Interestingly, Jacobs explains extensively that she is not against high-rise as such. She mentions Rockefeller Center as an example of a high-rise project which can be considered an enrichment of urban life and vitality. While many high-rise projects in New York of the mid-20th century resulted in a loss of the relationship between the street and the building, she shows that Rockefeller Center maintains and even enhances this relationship. The original street network was respected, and the ground floor of the complex is still today filled with shops, bars, theatres and other public and street-oriented amenities, while the center of the complex has become an important public space.

It is funny to read in Sigfried Giedion's book *Space, Time, Architecture* that he also considers the Rockefeller Center as a triumph of urban architecture – however as a triumph of Modernist urban architecture. He hopes that New York will grow with more projects like Rockefeller Center in the future. There is only one negative point in Rockefeller Center, says Giedion: the many street-oriented amenities, which he considers an undesirable continuation of the traditional city. He hopes that this street-orientation in high-rise blocks will disappear in the future.

This difference in appreciation of the relationship between high-rise buildings and the ground floor of the city is still one of the most crucial elements in the debate on high-rises in the city. It is this point that is being used in arguing *for* high-rise: this is the tool that will help intensify and vitalize the city, for densification is a condition for a sustainable city.

This is exactly what this book wants to address and discuss: in what way can high-rise really be regarded as a constructive contribution to sustainable cities? We can define sustainability as an approach that leaves our environment in the same condition – or in any case, not worse but preferably better off – for our children. Building high-rise projects that result in desolate urban districts which are demolished after a while is not a very effective contribution to a sustainable city. But high-rise buildings that enhance the vitality of the city, creating conditions for many different types of use, for differentiation, variation, flexibility and changes, is something that a city needs to survive as a city.

When the use of high-rise also contributes to the conservation of landscapes for nature development and recreation, it contributes even more to sustainability. And when it also contributes to a reduction of traffic, CO_2

emissions and energy costs, and to a reduced and more efficient use of building materials, it would really make sense. The question of whether high-rise really can play a substantial role in creating advantageous conditions for sustainable cities is the subject of this book. The contributors to this book provide the first attempts at answers.

In the first part of this book, the implications of high-rise for a sustainable city will be discussed. The authors in this part focus on the issue of defining under which conditions urban form can be considered sustainable and in which way high-rise can contribute to sustainable urban form. The second part focuses on understanding the processes of transformation and area development within cities necessary for urban densification and for making high-rise buildings possible. The big question here is if it is possible to develop high-rise projects without disturbing city life too much. Finally, the design of the buildings themselves as sustainable constructions, contributing to a healthy indoor and outdoor environment, and to a reduction of materials, energy and costs, will be discussed.

If it is possible to develop high-rise buildings that play a positive role with respect to all three aspects, only then can we say that we have entered a new era in the world of high-rise.

High-rise and the Sustainable City

1
High-rise Buildings and Sustainable Urban Form

Peter Bosselmann

ABSTRACT The question of whether high-rise buildings contribute to sustainable urban form could quite simply be answered with "yes", if it were not for the broad and vague definitions of the terms sustainable and urban. The term sustainable is no longer confined to the field of economics. In the present-day context, the question: "Do high-rise buildings contribute to sustainable urban form?" is like asking: "Do high-rise buildings contribute to the public good?" Equally in need of definition are the terms urban, urbanism and urbanity. In the literature, these terms describe the social conditions of life in cities, where people are supposedly tolerant and open to the world, as opposed to life in the country, or even the province, where life is supposedly more introverted and less diverse. However, for members of the design community the terms urban, urbanity and urbanism are used almost interchangeably and describe attributes of physical space with a high degree of spatial definition or containment. Designers see people's intensity of activities as a result of well-designed physical form. Only a qualified response would be useful. I will dissect the question and respond by presenting two arguments at two different levels: Are high-rise buildings sustainable, and do high-rises contribute to urbanity?

Office towers versus low-rise office parks

fig. 1 Concentration of high-rise office towers in San Francisco

In 1984 California's largest corporation, Chevron, vacated two 40 story office towers in downtown San Francisco and relocated to a low-rise office park at the former rural fringe of the San Francisco Bay Area. The company was not alone, the nation's largest telecommunication company made the same move to a neighboring site, so did the regional headquarter of a foreign car manufacturer. These companies were not trendsetters; suburban office parks have a long history (Mozingo, 2011). Also, such corporate exodus was not confined to suburban California; similar relocations took place in most metropolitan regions in North America. The reasons for companies to move from downtown locations to the suburban fringe

fig. 1

fig. 2   San Ramon office park
fig. 3a   Diagram of a Polycentric Region

were associated with the automation of corporate office operations that took place in the 1980s. Data processing could happen in locations with lower real estate values. No longer was it necessary for corporations to maintain a significant presence in highly accessible locations. Members of the public would no longer have to come in person as communication had taken the form of electronic file transfers that needed analysis and storage. The exact decision where to move was made by senior management and corporate board members, who preferred locations in the vicinity of their homes in semi-rural settings, locations where management already lived and where they sent their children to reputable suburban schools. →fig. 1, 2

fig. 2

The 4500 Chevron office workers had to follow. No longer would they take regional transit to work, which in downtown San Francisco functions like a subway with direct pedestrian connections to high-rise office towers. At the new location, the small former rural community of San Ramon, office workers had no choice but to drive and leave their car in the office park's vast parking lot for the remainder of the day. Here, Chevron and a number of companies had relocated to a former ranch. The landowners notified the county that they were taking steps towards incorporating as an independent municipality and applied to convert additional agricultural land for residential use of predominantly single family homes. The

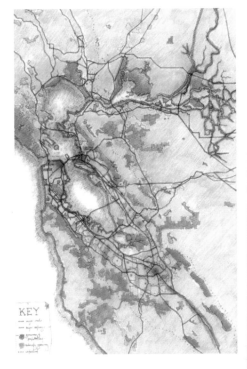

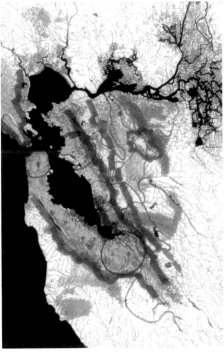

fig. 3a

fig. 3b

argument was made that more land was needed to provide housing for the new working population.

The process described here repeated itself not only in one geographic location; it radiated outwards from the historic employment centers of the San Francisco Bay Area to produce a polycentric metropolitan region of fifteen such centers. →fig. 3a,b

fig. 3b Diagram of a Polycentric Region

An early critique of North America's predominant vision for large metropolitan areas was written by Anthony Downs (1989). In his analysis, Downs did not use the term unsustainable to characterize the current vision for large metropolitan areas. The term was not in use as much as it is today. Nor did he point to the inefficient use of energy or the high carbon emissions that make the move from high-rise office towers to low-rise office parks unsustainable in our current assessment. But both factors are implicit in his critique about the major flaws of the North American vision for dispersed regions.

According to Downs, the first major flaw of the typical American vision was that it produced excessive travel; the second, that it had no housing provision for a broader range of income groups including lower paid workers that are essential for the functioning of any economy; thirdly, there was no consensus on how to finance infrastructure fairly; fourthly, there was no mechanism for resolving inevitable conflicts between the welfare of society as whole and the welfare of geographically small parts of society.

Remedies necessary for the repair of the metropolitan vision called for at least moderate high-density, especially of housing, but also for workplaces to be closer to where people live, thus a better integration of land use. His new vision preserves local authority, but within a framework that compels local government to act responsibly to meet regional needs, and his vision contains incentives that encourage individuals and households to take a more realistic account of the collective costs of their behavioural choices.

In answering the first question – are high-rise buildings more sustainable than the low-rise office park alternatives? – the answer is clearly positive, especially if all costs are taken into consideration, including the cost of infrastructure to support a polycentric configuration, the cost of housing for lower paid workers, the cost of energy consumed by the individual driver, and the costs associated with unsustainable practices, like increased carbon emission. However, on the balance sheet of the corporation, the move from high-rise towers to low-rise office parks has proven to be highly sustainable over the last 30 years.

The senior management at Chevron that decided on the 1984 move has retired. We can only speculate what new senior management will decide about Chevron's future location. For example, could the office park in San Ramon go up for sale, if Chevron were to move to Houston, Texas, where the petroleum industry could consolidate its political influence? I am not saying that Chevron should or will make such a move, but what is illustrated by the Chevron example is the fact that the work performed there is not tied to a building form or even a specific place.

The example also underlines that the Chevron situation is not unique to North America. In the European literature, Francois Ascher described urban regions defined by mobility (1995). Societies have so heavily invested in transportation, infrastructure and private communication that they have transformed profoundly at all levels. It's no use denying that the dispersed city form and all aspects of dispersed living have become the prevailing urban condition, not only in North America, but also in Europe. City designers now need to deal creatively with the dispersed city and shift their focus, at least partially, from the historic core of cities to city regions in order to reduce social and environmental fragmentation. This appeal for a new creativity at the regional scale was Thomas Sieverts' main argument in *Zwischenstadt* (1997), which was translated into: *Cities without Cities* (2003). The theme of a diffused urban form was also addressed by Bernardo Secchi in *La città del ventesimo secolo* (2005), and in his earlier work *Il raconto urbanistico*.

The role of high-rise towers in the current discussion about sustainable urban form is caught between those who advocate an ecological or landscape urbanism (Waldheim, 2006) and those who advocate compact urban form as in the new urbanism or the "cities for people" urbanism. The former group attempts to repair the wasteful consumption of land by reintroducing the ecological conditions that existed prior to the occurrence of low intensity use. The latter group emphasizes the need for higher density and better integration of activities that would lead to a reduction of automobile travel, greater walkability, and more public life in cities. High-rise buildings have less importance in the discussion about the former, more in the latter.

We therefore need to clarify the second question: Are high-rise buildings consistent with our understanding of good urban form?

Within Paris many districts enjoy more urban life than La Défense. The filmmaker Jacques Tati (1907–82) would have agreed. He lampooned the urbanity of the "forest of high buildings", as the Parisians referred to the office concentration outside the center of Paris. In fact, La Défense was invented to provide relief from the pressure to construct high-rise buildings in the center of Paris, such as had already occurred with the tower at Montparnasse station. In Rotterdam, towers like the Montevideo skyscraper provide a wonderful feeling of city life when inside on one of the upper floors looking out over the city and harbor, but at ground level, the building is very unpleasant to be next to.

Like the term sustainable, urbanism is a broad concept that has evolved over time. Louis Wirth, the prominent sociologist of the Chicago School, said that urbanism is not primarily spatial, nor is it positive in all of its dimensions (Wirth, 1938). Wirth's emphasis was that life in the urban community informed all structures of human behavior. Two criteria defining urbanism he explicitly stated were heterogeneity and density of people. Two additional criteria he implied: a person living in a city lives predominantly among strangers and city dwellers are subject to the dynamics of change, and thus feel the pulse of time more so than people of the countryside. Also for Jane Jacobs matters of urbanity were not primarily spatial. When talking about urbanity she describes conditions of vitality and social diversity (Jacobs, 1991). Designers influenced by Jacobs have contemplated how physical design can produce urbanism to a high degree by giving strength to the quality of life in inner city districts. The definition of urbanism has evolved in the context of sustainability to describe a compact urban form that reduces or eliminates residents' dependency on the automobile, encourages walking and bicycling, shared amenities, and reduces consumption of energy for heating or cooling apartments with shared walls versus those in free standing structures.

fig. 4 Integrated building typologies

However, for contemporary American society – largely raised in suburbs – to fully appreciate a high density social urbanism, cities must increase the quality and quantity of well-planned public spaces that are human in scale, healthy, safe and lively (Rogers, 2010).

Yet the relationship of high-rise buildings to the quality of adjacent public spaces is frequently associated with a number of flaws. More frequently high structures meet the ground with gravity instead of grace. In windy cities, high buildings channel high wind velocities from higher altitudes down to street level, where pedestrians and bicyclist struggle through gusts and colder temperatures (Bosselmann, 1998). Yes, tall buildings offer views, but they also block views, direct light and sunshine.

In North American downtown locations, where office towers can be tightly spaced, and are permitted to contain large floors areas without access to direct light, high-rise structures accommodate a significantly higher density of workplaces, when compared to low-rise office parks. However, for residential towers a different logic applies. Here tower separation rules will reduce residential density below that of mid-rise structures that are configured in rows to form city blocks. When

fig. 4

compared to a compact four story building – the height advocated by Christopher Alexander (1977) and others – and certainly to eight story buildings configured around the perimeter of a city block, high-rise structures do not accommodate higher residential density.

However, when carefully configured, the integration of high-rise towers can activate public life in cities (Macdonald, 2005). This is best done by first thinking about the character of the adjacent streets. Especially important is the design of the pedestrian realm. To entice people to walk, city streets should have active building frontages at ground level. But it is rarely ever possible to line all street frontages with ground level retail stores. Even in high density neighborhoods commercial frontages are confined to concentrations along selected city streets. Even if it were possible to use the lower floors of buildings for commercial uses, including workplaces, much of the building frontage at ground level would need to accommodate residential uses. Here, a transition zone is needed to protect the privacy of those who live on lower floors from those who walk or drive by. Instead of entering the high-rise tower through a common lobby, residents who live in the lower floors of high-rise structures could enter their units directly from the streets. Like residents who live on a street lined with individual row houses, they would walk up a few steps onto a private stoop and enter their home after passing through a private transition zone designed like a terrace. The configuration described here is illustrated in Figure 4. →fig. 4 The illustration shows a high-rise tower that is integrated with other building types, including three or four story townhouse structures.

Finally then, if so many qualifiers are necessary to justify high-rise construction, why are we having this discussion? There must be another reason for building them. As structures, high-rise buildings can be an excellent financial proposition for investors and for others high-rise structures can be symbols. Most high-rise buildings have a highly functional appearance and transmit very little symbolic importance. However, the array of curious building shapes that emerged during the first decade of the millennium in Shanghai might have been inspirational and have led to proposals for twisted shapes in other largely horizontal cityscapes like St. Petersburg,

fig. 5a San Francisco Skyline in 2005
fig. 5b San Francisco Skyline with approved
  and considered projects prior to 2008

London, Milan, Malmo, Paris, Berlin and Vienna. Contemporary modelling tools certainly make it possible to conceive fluid shapes with great ease. The shapes are selected for their novelty as symbols and they become the focus of attention.

Symbols have their own associated risks. In order to enter the collective consciousness, symbols are in need of interpretation as a reference to an idea or concept. As the Swiss linguist Ferdinand de Saussure (1857–1913) pointed out, "the connection between the signifier and the signified is arbitrary." For symbols to be understood they need to be grounded, because the shape of a symbol neither resembles nor is causally connected to its reference. Meaning depends upon agreement, upon a shared convention. However, the large volume and height of tall structures has far greater consequences on urban conditions than the structure as a symbol. As symbols high-rise buildings might wane, or even be ridiculed, but once entitled as projects and built, high-rise buildings become a commodity (Bosselmann, 2008).

The reader may have noticed that implicit in my arguments is the advocacy for rules and regulations that define the size and placement of high structures, their locations and how high buildings relate to the city at ground level. Large North American cities boast skylines defined by their high-rise buildings. In New York the skyline forms a ridge with peaks and saddles along the center line of Manhattan. Figure 1 illustrates San Francisco's skyline configurations. Since the early 1970s the

fig. 5a,b

distribution of high-rise structures follows the configuration of a hill, a constructed hill compatible with the city's natural topography. Radiating from a peak at the center of the financial district, the height of skyscrapers diminishes until allowable building heights are similar to those of the adjacent neighborhoods. The so-called "downtown hill policy" has governed high-rise development in San Francisco for nearly 40 years. It has resulted in a concentration that can more readily be served by transit than a spread out distribution. The financial district is highly walkable thus encouraging the use of transit. Importantly, the concentrated form has had an effect on land values, and therefore land speculation. Areas adjacent to the downtown core can remain available for small professional firms and services because land values have been based on a lower utilization of the land than those a few blocks away in the core area where high-rise buildings are permitted.

Given San Francisco's generally high land values small professional offices and services would be pushed out of the city without an effective bridle on the distribution of high-rise development. Figure 5 illustrates the San Francisco skyline prior to 2005 →fig. 5a and the amount and distribution of high-rise development entitled, or seriously considered prior to 2008, →fig. 5b during the building boom years prior to the financial crisis.

The topic of high-rise buildings and sustainable urbanism can easily lead to a multifaceted discussion. The pioneering structural engineer Fazlur Khan (1929–1982) of the Chicago School of Architecture, who is well known for his innovative designs of high-rise structures, contributed some wisdom early on: designing high-rise structures is as much an engineering challenge as it is a social and political concern.

REFERENCES

— Alexander, Christopher *et al.* 1977. "Pattern 21: Four Story Limit," *Pattern Language, Towns Buildings Construction.* New York: Oxford University Press.

— Ascher, Francois 1995. *Métapolis on l'avenir des villages.* Edition Odile Jacob.

— Bosselmann, Peter 1998. *Representation of Places, reality and realism in city design.* Berkeley: UC Press.

— Bosselmann, Peter 2008. *Urban Transformation, understanding city design and form.* Washington DC: Island Press.

— Downs, Anthony 1989. "The Need for a New Vision for the Development of Large US Metropolitan Areas," in a study commissioned by Solomon Brothers. Washington DC, Brookings Institution.

— Jacobs, Jane 1991. *Life and Death of Great American Cities.* New York: Random House.

— Macdonald, Elizabeth 2005. "Street-Facing Dwelling Units and Livability: The Impacts of Emerging Building Types in Vancouver's New High-Density Residential Neighbour-hoods," *Journal of Urban Design* 10:1, pp. 13-38.

— Mozingo, Louise 2011. Pastoral Capitalism, a History of Suburban Corporate Landscapes. Cambridge Mass.: MIT Press.

— Rogers, Richard 2010. Forward in Cities for People by Jan Gehl. Washington DC: Island Press.

— Sieverts, Thomas 1997. Zwischenstadt, zwischen Ort und Welt Raum und Zeit Stadt und Land. Sieverts, Thomas 2003 translation. Cities Without Cities: An interpretation of the Zwischenstadt, New York: Taylor and Francis.

— Secchi, Bernardo 2005. La città del ventesimo secolo. Rome: Laterza.

— Waldheim, Charles 2006. The Landscape Urbanism Reader. New York: Princeton Architectural Press.

— Wirth, Lois 1938. "Urbanism As A Way of Life," in AJS 44, pp. 1-24.

IMAGE SOURCES

— {fig. 1} Photo by Judith Stilgenbauer
— {fig. 2} Microsoft BING, Terraserver
— {fig. 5} Bosselmann, Parker

2
High-rise – Genesis and Exodus of a Type

Markus Appenzeller

This story is a personal one. It might not fully comply with what science may say but it offers a way of reading developments – back then, now and in the future. It is a my personal diary on high-rise.

Back in the late 1990s when I was still studying and about to leave for a year in Chicago, one of my teachers recommended a book as preparation. Its title: *The Pig and the Skyscraper – a History of our Future,* by Italian socialist writer Marco d'Eramo. A cryptic title for an impressive story about how the skyscraper came about, what its drivers were and why all this happened for the first time in Chicago. To give a short answer: it was the meatpacking industry and the railway with its cooled carriages – the emergence of capitalism in its most pure form and the

fig. 1

fig. 1   Tower types
fig. 2   Chicago Tribune
          Tower
fig. 3   Chicago Tribune
          Tower, Gropius
          Design
fig. 4a   Chicago Tribune
          Tower, Saarinen
          Design
fig. 4b   Chicago Tribune
          Tower, Loos Design

fig. 3

fig. 2

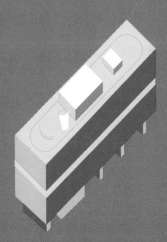

fig. 4a,b

fig. 5 **The Woolworth Building**

fact that the "windy city" was and still is the crossroads of the United States. For the first time in history scarcity of land, technology and the ego of investors and architects created a critical mass for the high-rise to emerge.

Shortly thereafter – it was in the Spring of 2000 while in Chicago – I stumbled across another important but less known event that took place in the same city. An architectural competition held by the Chicago Tribune. →fig. 1,2,3,4a,b By that time it was the biggest newspaper of the city and one of the most important ones in the entire USA. In 1922 they invited architects from all over the world to join an international design competition for a tower that was supposed to become "the most beautiful and eye-catching building in the world" – their future headquarters. What is not so important about that story is the winning entry – a design by John Mead Howells and Raymond Hood in the neo-Gothic style popular around the time. The much more interesting part is the range of entries contributed by some of the most renowned architects of the time. Gropius, Saarinen, the Luckhard brothers, Richard Mine and many others sent in proposals.

fig. 5

The most radical one is probably the entry by Adolf Loos – a gigantic Doric column mutated into a building.

The competition and especially the different renderings showed that by that time typologically the world had already developed two types of high-rise buildings. They responded to the different urban conditions that could be found in Europe and the United States and show the clash of urban cultures that had developed in the old and the new world. While most European cities had grown organically over centuries, American ones had been planned and grown to metropolitan scale within a short time. European cities were based on an axis and important iconic buildings. The American city was based on the grid where hierarchy of buildings was achieved by widening the street and creating a plaza or simply by the scale of the building. Subsequently in the entries of European architects the high-rise was an icon that stood on its own like the churches and palaces did in history. It was an icon to be placed in key locations on an axis. The entries of many American architects showed towers that were different: a city block with a part extruded, a high building in a row of buildings. This can best be seen in some of the skyscrapers built around the time in New York with the Woolworth Building as the archetype. →fig. 5

In 2008 I went to the Cote d'Azur together with my family. Not to see architecture but to enjoy the beaches with the kids. But of course – if one is in Marseille anyway then… – well, we went to see the Unité d'Habitation →fig. 6 designed in 1952 by Le Corbusier. It was a moving experience. A slab type high-rise where pedestrian streets were lifted into the air, where the roof was programmed with kindergarten and swimming pool and where the little store on the 9th level still provided probably the same selection of food it did when the building was completed. The other shops in the meantime had been taken over by followers of Corbu. They are easy to recognize since they wear the same glasses as the master. This building is a different kind of high-rise, a slab type with a mix of uses on higher levels.

As a discovery tour of high-rises, we can summarize three different types:
a) the American high-rise, built in a row;
b) the European high-rise, a free standing icon;
c) the inventions of Le Corbusier.

fig. 6 The Unité d'Habitation

fig. 7 Diagram Cross fertilization
fig. 8 Burj Khalifa

All other buildings refer back to these archetypes and it is these three archetypes that were sent on a tour around the world in the last 70 years – with stops in Europe, East Asia and the Persian Gulf. In all these places they mutated and in each of these places the conditions found on the ground are the defining factors for the type of mutation. →fig. 7

Fall 2008: in the Persian Gulf incredible amounts of money met a barely existing urban culture and low pressure from the demographic side. A people that until half a century ago had largely lived in Bedouin tents, had become rich by exploiting the oil wells in the region, and had erected nothing other than enormous, autonomous tents, have culminated – at this point anyway – with the Burj Khalifa. →fig. 8

Technically this building might be a masterpiece of engineering and as an icon demonstrating ego and ambition it might work – though this is highly questionable at present. What is interesting when looking at this super-iconic mutation of the European style high-rise is that the sheer size leads to a mixed use building and a structure where what could be considered public (or publically accessible) space has been lifted into the sky. It remains to be seen if these public floors will develop into spaces of a particular, unprecedented quality, but for the first time they exist on a larger scale.

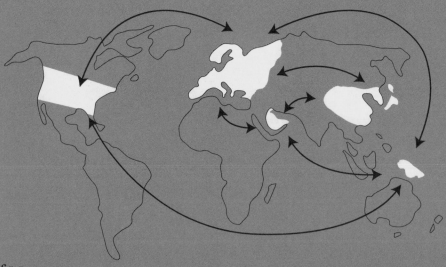

fig. 7

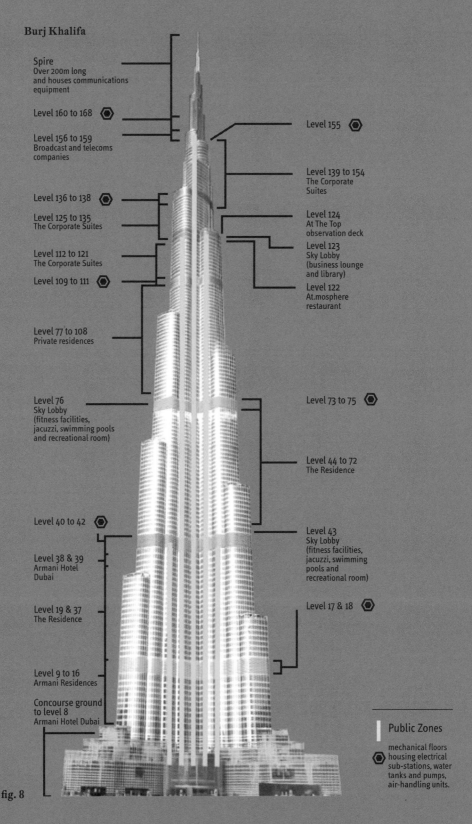

Burj Khalifa

Spire
Over 200m long
and houses communications
equipment

Level 160 to 168 ⬡

Level 156 to 159
Broadcast and telecoms
companies

Level 136 to 138 ⬡

Level 125 to 135
The Corporate Suites

Level 112 to 121
The Corporate Suites

Level 109 to 111 ⬡

Level 77 to 108
Private residences

Level 76
Sky Lobby
(fitness facilities,
jacuzzi, swimming pools
and recreational room)

Level 40 to 42 ⬡

Level 38 & 39
Armani Hotel
Dubai

Level 19 & 37
The Residence

Level 9 to 16
Armani Residences

Concourse ground
to level 8
Armani Hotel Dubai

Level 155 ⬡

Level 139 to 154
The Corporate
Suites

Level 124
At The Top
observation deck

Level 123
Sky Lobby
(business lounge
and library)

Level 122
At.mosphere
restaurant

Level 73 to 75 ⬡

Level 44 to 72
The Residence

Level 43
Sky Lobby
(fitness facilities,
jacuzzi, swimming
pools and
recreational room)

Level 17 & 18 ⬡

Public Zones

⬡ mechanical floors
housing electrical
sub-stations, water
tanks and pumps,
air-handling units.

fig. 8

fig. 9   Hyperbuilding
fig. 10 CCTV
fig. 11 Steven Holl Modern
fig. 12 Belle van Zuylen
fig. 13 Tour signal
fig. 14 Steven Holl Modern

In the Summer of 2009 I repeatedly went to China. Particularly there, but also in the rest of East Asia, reasonable amounts of funds are available but in contrast to the Gulf, an urban culture exists, has done for a long time and cities are facing enormous population growth. This leads to unprecedented densities and land values with the high-rise often as the only possible solution. Here I am not talking about the omnipresent residential compounds that can be found in all Chinese cities. This is about the key locations in these cities. Locations where complexity (roads, public transport, existing but small amounts of open space...) is a given condition and any building has to deal with it. This lends itself almost naturally to hybrid buildings →fig. 9 or ensembles thereof. On the intersection of two metro lines and adjacent to a motorway ramp are a shopping mall with restaurants and a rooftop park, a hotel and several office towers and condominium high-rises combined with a large parking garage, a karaoke club, a community center and a myriad of restaurants. Not only do these buildings stop being readable as autonomous structures, they also combine all three archetypes of towers and in their almost endless recombination form interesting collective hybrids that resemble 3D cities

fig. 9

fig. 10

fig. 11

from science fiction movies. Prominent examples are the Hyper Building projected for Bangkok and CCTV →fig. 10 in Beijing designed by OMA or Steven Holl's MoMA Modern II →fig. 11 in the same city.

February 2011: Back in Europe on a grey winter day – in a region where demographic pressure has ceased to exist, a wealthy region and a region with an urban tissue largely defined by mid-size cities of 200,000–700,000 inhabitants. Here the high-rise in most cases is not the most obvious choice, but it is a choice that can create a unique selling point in a highly competitive real estate market and it is a choice that caters to the desires of a growing number of people wanting to live in the centers of these cities again. In the Netherlands we have been learning from the results that have been generated in the East and South of our continent – or better – we have been part of the perpetual cross fertilization that globalization has led to. European-scale super icons have been proposed, such as the Belle van Zuylen tower →fig. 12 in Leidsche Rijn, designed by De Architekten Cie. High-rise buildings with quasi-public spaces on higher levels have been proposed such as the Tour Signal →fig. 13 by Jean Nouvel

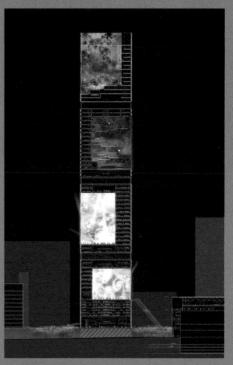

fig. 13

fig. 12

fig. 14

fig. 15 Bishopsgate Goods Yard
fig. 16 Wijnhaven
fig. 17 Tower types
fig. 18 Red Apple

for La Défense in Paris. And also European versions of the collective hybrid such as the De Rotterdam Building →fig. 14 by OMA are under construction. But all of them are mini-versions of their Arabic and Asian counterparts and are more the result of political will than immediate market necessity.

In the future, high-rise in Europe will really be less about the buildings themselves, than about the combination or composition of high-rises. This "curation" of towers that form ensembles together create a critical mass for a more intense urban life. There are numerous examples where the aim to cluster individual high-rise buildings has led to quality results. There have been a series of proposals

3d-Guidelines: Envelope Generation

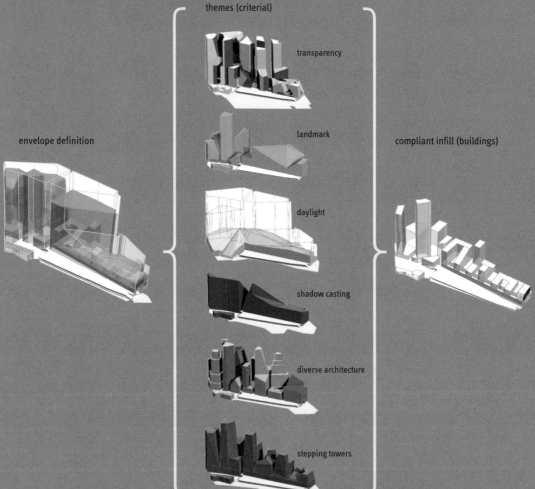

envelope definition

themes (criterial)

transparency

landmark

daylight

shadow casting

diverse architecture

stepping towers

compliant infill (buildings)

fig. 15

fig. 16

for a coordinated approach such as the "city crown" idea of Bruno Taut and the proposal for a ring of high-rises around the center of Stuttgart by Ernst Otto Oswald. Today Rotterdam's Wijnhaven Island, →fig. 15,16,17,18 the area around Liverpool Street Station in London →fig. 19 and La Défense →fig.20 in Paris can serve as examples for successful curatorship that moved the focus away from the individual building towards an overall massing strategy for all of them. It is this approach that still makes European city skylines appear different than elsewhere.

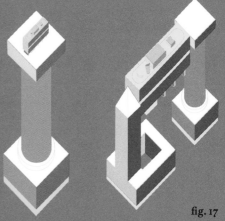

fig. 17

fig. 18

fig. 19   Skyline London
fig. 20   La Defense, France

What form the high-rise will take next remains pure speculation. The CCTV project showed that you can be extremely iconic without being extremely high. The Burj Khalifa demonstrated that technically virtually any height one can afford is possible and with the market economy increasingly dictating what cities can or cannot do, any curatorial high-rise concept can be jeopardized quickly. Maybe the discussion should not focus on high-rise as an autonomous type anymore. Maybe the type as such is a Modernist concept we all should seek to overcome and we should develop hybrids for the benefit of the liveliness and complexity of our cities and for the benefit of our creative potential as designers and users of urban spaces equally.

IMAGE SOURCES

— {fig. 1} tower types, Author
— {fig. 2} Chicago Tribune Tower: http://2.bp.blogspot.
  com/_1lDkgkbkQmA/TI1QAEuSJHI/AAAAAAAABpQ/ reH3jC-
  oyUGY/s1600/downtown+sunday+003.JPG
— {fig. 3} Chicgao Tribune Tower Gropius Design: http://www.
  yatzer.com/assets/Article/1831/images/
  Bauhaus_A-Conceptual-Model_The_Exhibition_Berlin_
  at_yatzer_1.jpg
— {fig. 4a} Chicago Tribune Tower Saarinen Design
  http://www.ou.edu/class/arch4443/Tribune%20Tower%20
  Competition/Second%20Prize.jpg
— {fig. 4b} Chicago Tribune Tower Loos Design
  http://www.eikongraphia.com/wordpress/wp-content/
  tribune_loos.jpg
— {fig. 5} Woolworth Building http://www.whitworthfamily.org/
  images/Woolworth-Bldg-NY-Commerce-01.jpg
— {fig. 6} Unite d'habitation, http://www.flickr.com/photos/
  jpmm/4182618008/sizes/o/in/photostream/
— {fig. 6} Cross fertilization, Author
— {fig. 8} Burj Khalifa, Diagram: author, basis:http://newsilike.files.
  wordpress.com/2010/12/jan2010worldtallestburjkhalifa.jpg
— Supericon, Author
— {fig. 9} Hyperbuilding, http://nicholashanna.com/wp-con-
  tent/uploads/2008/02/picture-1.png
— {fig. 10} CCTV, http://media.photobucket.com/image/
  cctv%20beijing/foglio23/14.jpg
— {fig. 11} Steven Holl Modern http://www.stevenholl.com/
  project-detail.php?id=58&type=&page=0
— {fig. 12} Belle van Zuylen, http://www.service-studieverenig-

fig. 19

fig. 20

ing.nl/images/Belle_van_Zuylen_juli_2008_exterior.jpg

— {fig. 13} Tour signal, http://static.worldarchitecturenews.
com/news_images/2370_4_Tour%20signal%204big.jpg

— {fig. 14} De Rotterdam, http://www.plataformaarquitectura.
cl/wp-content/uploads/2009/07/exterior-night-de-
rotterdam.jpg

— {fig. 15} Bishopsgate Goods Yard KCAP Architects&Planners

— {fig. 16} Wijnhaven, KCAP Architects&Planners

— {fig. 17} tower types, Author

— {fig. 18} Red Apple, KCAP Architects&Planners

— {fig. 19} Skyline London http://upload.wikimedia.org/
wikipedia/commons/f/f6/City_of_London_skyline_from_
London_City_Hall_-_Oct_2008.jpg

— {fig. 20} La Defense, http://www.graefmultimedia.
nl/105%20

3
European Approaches to Managing Higher Densities and Higher Buildings: London's Ascendancy

Lora Nicolaou

ABSTRACT The high-rise building is not a traditional building form associated with European cities. Historically, with a few exceptions, tall developments in Europe were not driven by comprehensive building height policies, but were a by-product of mass social housing delivered after the Second World War and the erection of individual, mainly office buildings, as landmarks in major commercial centres. This is in contrast with American and Asian cities where tall developments are far more prevalent and clustered.

Recently the interests in high buildings has re-emerged in Europe. The main drivers relate to the aspirations of places in developing an international image coupled with commercial demands. Secondary is the intention to increase urban density in line with the latest policy on sustainability. Although tall buildings have merits in these areas, their development needs to be cautiously evaluated against the attributes of the place (physical, social and economic) and environmental impact.

The current debates on tall development in the UK, centred in London, although extensive, often fails to address in detail specific issues of impact and long term value as an accommodation model of the future. This paper aims to highlight urban planning and design issues associated with tall developments in order to inform current debates and discussions on setting up new policies or evaluating development proposals in the context of traditional cities. London is used as a central reference.

The increased interest in tall buildings since the late 1990s continues to puzzle me. The trend seemed to me at the time a temporary fashion, nothing more than a renewed fascination with a relatively "old-fashioned" building type. Being involved in drafting policies and working with developers on tall building projects, I became increasingly aware of the challenges experienced by planning authorities and the development industry alike, to make on the one hand the feasibility of such buildings work (particularly in locations of lower land value) and on the other the efforts put in by designers and planners to integrate their scale and particularities in existing traditional places. More than a decade and a half later, and the fascination shows no signs of abating. On the contrary, tall buildings are beginning to change the shape of cities, particularly in the UK and more decisively the City of London.

Given the mounting pressure for more and taller development, not only in metropolitan regions but small towns and cities, there has been little development in a shared understanding of the implications that arise from the implementation of tall developments, and to date there are very few authorities with mature strategies or tested tall building policies. Past experience is not particularly helpful: tall buildings from the 1960s and 1970s were mainly instances of sub-Corbusian high-rise housing, driven primarily by housing policy and the public sector reconstruction programmes, often built on sites with no particularly locational or environmental characteristics that lent themselves to building tall. The Modernist urban model of "buildings in landscape" reflected the design culture of the times and was informed by arguments of social reconstruction. In contrast contemporary pressures seem to be driven purely by private sector demand for higher densities (and profit), regulated – if at all – by relatively weak policies and with very little "post occupancy" evaluation research to inform their past performance and evidence of success and longer term value.

fig. 1 The "Walkie Talkie" at 20 Fenchurch
Street by Rafael Viñoly

Recent demand for taller and larger development seems to also defy a "spatial logic" and ignores conventional building/property economics. Large scale, high value commercial space traditionally found itself in central metropolitan office locations. More recently tall commercial buildings are also proposed in marginal office locations not only in metropolitan regions but in small cities and towns with low or even no demand for prime office space. The development risks relating to both the type of space and amount of accommodation to be provided make the relationship between commercial logic of such development and current planning policy difficult to square (DEGW, 2002; GLA, SDS 19, 2002). While tall commercial buildings are only (if at all) feasible in city centres or high value commercial nodes, tall residential buildings are proposed (particularly during the economic boom of the last 10 years) literary everywhere. Because of this haphazard nature of demand, planning authorities of unprepared particularly smaller cities and towns are forced to adopt "preventative" more than "proactive" development control policies with obvious shortcomings.

In drafting new land-use policies with tall buildings in mind there is little guidance to borrow from previous practice or other places. US and Asian zoning plans and guidelines refer to the "tall building" as the "theme" and the basic ingredient of the downtown morphology and have developed over the years sophisticated guidance regulations. Equivalent European policies which emerged after the war, such as the one for Rotterdam centre and the Frankfurt office quarter, initially defined zones with very broad, if at all, design prescriptions (DEGW 1998). Both cities are beginning to re-evaluate the impact of the "outline" prescriptions in their policies, proposing now a more detailed regulation for future development.

Most of the other cities with no references to tall buildings in their policies after the war, began to address the issue in the 1990s, as one of individual urban "insertions", rather than considering it as a fundamental comprehensive transformation of city districts. Cities like London continue to "judge" each planning application on the basis of its merit and impact on its surroundings with no assumptions of adjacent similar projects. Inevitably this leads to compromised environmental standards, if one is interested in accommodating more and more unplanned buildings in the same location.

One other pertinent question is the one of "fit" in European cities where pressure for more space (and taller buildings) coincides with pressures for conservation of the built environment. Ironically, user research associated with the tall buildings policy research commissioned by the Mayor of London indicates that it is the value generated by the cultural and environmental quality of the city's historic cores that leads to the high value demand and in turn associated demand for larger

fig. 1

and taller developments (DEGW, 2000). The debate on urban change and when a "heritage site" becomes a "contemporary" business distinct is polarised. An example of how this debate unfolded in London, where tall buildings shifted to the top of the political agenda, took place when there was a call for an inquiry by the Secretary of State on 20 Fenchurch Street, a building designed by Rafael Viñoly, and supported by the City of London →fig. 1 Threats from UNESCO to withdraw the City's status as an international Heritage Site, led to endless political debates with no substantive research or professional inputs supporting positions, rendering such debates opinion rather than evidence-based. They produce again and again inconclusive, valid only in individual cases and extremely expensive responses to a continuing demand for more such developments.

The understanding of the range of terms of reference presented in this paper derives from an extensive portfolio of policy research, townscape guidance, master planning and tall buildings briefing and design that urban planners DEGW has been involved with since the mid-1990s. Policy research included strategies for Rotterdam, Dublin and London. Follow-up projects triggered by obvious and pressing demand for taller buildings across the UK and Ireland included the development of tools and design rationales which positioned density and building height of new developments in their context.

Strategic consideration of policy frameworks

The approach to any planning issue is critically informed by the definition of the condition it wants to address. Many planning policy discussions in the UK, seem reactive rather than proactive beginning from a position of "why not", leading to the adoption of policies that are relevant to other places, based on superficial evaluation and not their appropriateness to place. Increased density and height can change fundamentally the character of cites in relatively short timescales and need to be based on a clear understanding of the necessity and "why" such a fundamental transformation would be constructive in the long term.

The "why" in different cities derives from different development drivers which are not only place but time specific. Rotterdam in the mid-1990s was fundamentally re-evaluating its city centre plan and attempted to establish a set of distinctive city centre quarters. Building design, townscape and "brand image" implications, became the focus of a revised policy on tall buildings and all in the context of low demand at the time. Dublin addressed the same issue in a very different context in the late 1990s. A key quest for the city was to decide how far the new reality of a continuously booming economy (Celtic Tiger) required a new city configuration, with implications on the type and quantity of space in the city centre and/or an expression of a new image. A radical turnaround would critically change the nature of Dublin as a low-rise city. Political and cultural opinions centred on how far changes should go: were they necessities (*i.e.* "have to") or desires (*i.e.* "want to"), these being often difficult to distinguish. In London the evaluation of pros and cons for taller buildings was prompted by a different concern: to what extent London might lose its economic position as a leading international financial centre, if planning policy was to restrict tall building particularly in the City of London. A parallel concern was the impact on conservation of the central business district's historic character, a unique international location, and on the integrity of London's Views policy.

Another condition which characterises debates is often the contradictory or inconclusive nature of the arguments. In London for example, where the demand for space supply (often a result of a restrictive planning policy) is identifiable, the demand for tall buildings is difficult to verify. User surveys at the time of the DEGW research into key economic sectors indicated that there was acute demand for large amounts of space in a single location, while the nature of space was not of a particular concern (single large building tall or short, a collection of buildings, etc.). Furthermore, the historic character of central London was noted as one of the most powerful criterion for the choice of the City of London as a preferred location (rather than Canary Wharf, Frankfurt or even New York), while the city was at the same time being threatened by an influx of a significant number of skyscraper applications. A survey of existing London skyscrapers

fig. 2 Meeting user priorities, City of London
buildings compared

revealed yet one other inconsistency. Most tall buildings fulfilled only a fraction of user requirements with serious shortcomings as a modern industry space model. →fig. 2

Arguments *for* and *against*

In most places tall buildings debates have focused on city macro and micro economics and the ability of architecture and development activity to change the image and branding of cities. Such regeneration pressures find different responses in each context reflecting the scale, city character and local culture. More specifically, arguments for and against which were derived from public consultation programmes in Rotterdam, London and Dublin were consistent as themes.

Views why high-rise might be appropriate were:
— Intensification of space and use in places with particularly extensive infrastructure capacity (transport service, social amenities, etc.);
— Global positioning and positive change of city image;
— Regeneration of places through positioning of large schemes and signposting of locations;
— Diversification of tenancies and encouragement of sectors outside existing demand (*i.e.* high-end service sectors in secondary locations);
— Investment advantages and promotion of development industry in locations that would otherwise not attract investment;
— Desire – pressure by "stakeholder" groups with reference to changes to city aesthetic quality in preferences toward the architecture of tall buildings.

The reasons "why not" focused on:
— Inefficiency of building type (utilisation of space as a result of extensive core in relation to total building footprint);
— Energy performance of skyscrapers which in general perform worse than conventional buildings with significant construction costs for improvement of performance;
— Limit to the impact of mixed use and tenure relating not only to physical characteristics of space and geometry of the plan but high rental and maintenance costs;

Tenants appreciation of tall building attributes

	34 St. Mary's Axe	Minerva Tower	London B Tower	51 Lime St.	122 Leadenhall St.	Heron Tower	City Tower
Support for distributed working Looser lease structures							
Mixed use		★		★			
Varied floor plates Aspect	★★	★	★★	★	★★	★	
Vertical ciro as experience Opening up the core mini atria, major atria	★	★★			★★	★★★	
Sustainable design features			★			★	
Hot spots eto							
Value ad ding services							
Building as a place Building as a brand	★★	★	★★		★		
Enhanced sense of place	★				★		

fig. 2

— Compromises of vitality and activity with a tendency for such buildings to "suck" activity inside rather than inject vitality into the public space;
— Negative impact on urban character as a result of the way tall buildings are positioned on the plot with extensive blank walls, service entrances to basement and single front entrance condition;
— Lack of development flexibility such as phasing of a building, future remodelling and redevelopment, etc.;
— Narrow sector demand relating to suitability of plan and affordability (particular economic sectors and residential clients), with potential impact of demographics if applied in a wide urban area.

Measuring the implications of the collective impact of larger developments or tall buildings is even more difficult to establish, particularly when policy (such as in the case of London) allows for incremental "demand based" delivery of buildings over a longer period. For example,

fig. 3 Increase of plot ratio density in relation
        to building height across a variety of
        housing typologies
fig. 4 Comparative capacity in building
        volume and population between
        Rotterdam and Paris Centres

where in a particular location transport impact is considered positive because of the utilisation of excess capacity, at another level localised congestion is being generated, thus compromising environmental quality. Similarly arguments concerning qualitative issues are rarely clear cut; in discussing the impact of architecture on city image and branding, it is almost impossible to derive a decisive strategy out of a number of contradicting often subjective and/or culturally biased views.

Policy research on the three cities' policies attempted to investigate some of these issues in a more substantive manner with focus on the three main debates: how far tall buildings assist cities with their intensification policies, whether one can verify the regeneration impact of larger development, and how far the brand value of architecture and image of such buildings suits cities and tenants.

Intensification and increased densities

The issue of height and scale is always associated with increased densities. It is worth noting that groups of tall

fig. 3

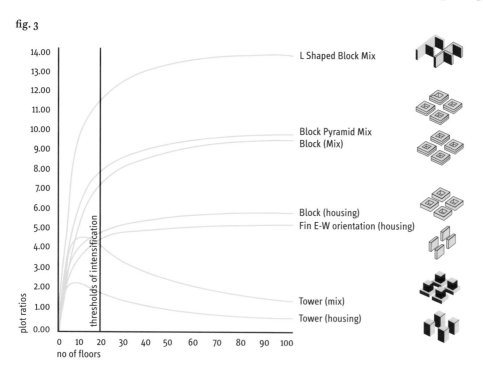

buildings or single tall buildings have very different effects on city growth and sustainability. Clusters of buildings can significantly increase densities of city neighbourhoods, have a bigger capacity to regenerate locations and can shift the economic base of places, simply through the scale of the intervention (if not its image change). In contrast, single tall buildings have mostly a landmark function. While it intensifies the "plot" (and associated revenue and land value), it does not have a significant impact on the capacity of the city block or city quarter.

Increasing density through increased height also has limitations and thresholds beyond which either density or environmental quality is compromised. Simple modelling →fig. 3 of different housing typologies, taking as a given a constant climatic performance, shows that density increases with height up to a point. Buildings need to be "spaced out" in order to allow for similar energy performance. Most housing models as indicated in Figure 1 seem to peak at around 20 storeys. Real place conditions bring added restrictions and will show further decreased potential for given building heights. It is also important to note that Asian and US models, which are based on fundamentally different environmental performance standards, have never been investigated in terms of their performance and are therefore difficult to use as benchmarks.

Validating the reality of urban models is very easily done through empirical measurement of real places. A comparison of city centre morphologies between Rotterdam and Paris →fig. 4 shows Parisian densities at 6:1 plot ratio and higher than Rotterdam densities which are 5:1. The

fig. 4

Rotterdam centre core: 1:5
The "ruit": 450,000 inhabitants

Paris centre core: 1:6
The "peripherique": 2.3 m. inhabitants

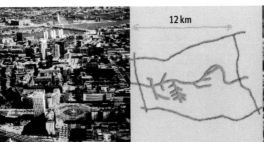
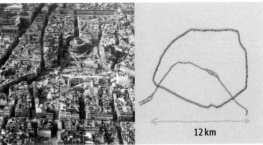

respective maximum buildings heights in the two city centres are 32 m and 150 m. Similarly the average density for the City of London of a 5:1 plot ration (with buildings up to 300m high) compares to the West End of London densities of 4:1 (dense 4–6 storeys terraced blocks). More importantly a comparison of population densities across Rotterdam and Paris shows the success of the latter to accommodate much larger populations within the same square mileage (2.3 million in Paris vs. 450,000 in Rotterdam). What is obvious from these simple measured indicators is that the comprehensive management of height and the choice of morphological models are decisive in achieving higher capacities. Intensification at a city-wide scale relies primarily on managing effectively land and infrastructure resources.

Impact on regeneration

To what extent tall buildings act as a catalyst for regeneration is a difficult question to answer on the basis of precedents. The evidence is clearly open to interpretation and scrutiny. Looking at examples of area regeneration such as Canary Wharf or Chelsea Harbour in London, Montmartre in Paris, Malmo in Sweden, it is difficult to say what the role of tall buildings was in the success of the plans' ambitions. Considering the scale, complexity and character of the master plans, it seems unlikely that the tall building elements kick-started change or were decisive in delivering the projects. In the cases of Chelsea Harbour or Montmartre, the tall buildings perhaps branded the individual development but clearly have done very little in regenerating the wider area which stayed largely undeveloped for decades after. In successful cases of city renewal a number of other preconditions seem to characterise major regeneration projects:
— they are large and part of comprehensively redeveloped frameworks
— they are supported by a strong policy and political support at the outset
— there is more often than not substantial infrastructure investment well beyond the development contributions locally (by central and local governments),
— they are associated with commitments to longer term (30 year) redevelopment programmes

A more recent research study by Colin Buchanan on the economic impact of tall buildings clearly verifies that shifts in the economic base of places is a result of the infrastructure improvements often associated with tall development more than the buildings themselves (Buchanan, 2008).

Brand value for cities and tenants

Most recent town centre regeneration arguments in the UK (Manchester, Leeds, Liverpool, etc.) regard taller buildings as a postmark of change but also as a tool for attracting a different type and higher value tenants. Its distinctive architecture has been used as a strong branding tool which during economic booms and in the short term, has been considered to be effective. In places with a longer experience in building tall, like Rotterdam, views are changing with concerns that Rotterdam is becoming "like everywhere else" with outdated tall buildings losing their brand value. Key developments are increasingly being characterised by international style architecture of not always great quality because of the relatively low land values the city experiences (compared to London, let's say). The city is shifting its emphasis now to the delivery of its public space programme in an attempt to improve environmental quality and make the city more attractive to businesses and its inhabitants. Examples such as Barcelona with its public space programme and Glasgow with its "Glasgow Smiles Better" campaign focusing on an events programme have clearly shown that city branding relies on more tactile and complex attributes.

Frankfurt is unique in Europe in having associated the skyscraper city form with its economic positioning. After the war the city designated a zone for taller buildings outside the traditional city centre core and attracted the relocation of the first bank in Frankfurt, at a time when the financial sector needed to express and celebrate its post-war economic regeneration success. Planners and historians still believe that the foresight of the local planning authority and local politicians that allowed bank headquarters in skyscrapers secured the city's fortunes.

fig. 5a Impact of morphology on built density.
        London: plot ratio 1:5.6
fig. 5b Impact of morphology on built density.
        Paris: plot ratio 1:6

To what extent tall tower buildings meet commercial or residential user priorities is a particularly neglected issue, with very little research by policy makers. Relevant concerns only refer to building efficiency and often within the framework of property evaluations. The case of housing reconstruction in the 1970s indicated the failure of many post-war public sector housing experiments. Initial assumptions after the 1970s suggested that the type of the building itself and the structure of space, was generating anti-social behaviours and was culturally inappropriate. Some tall buildings were demolished as a result. These ideas are very quickly changing with building refurbishments coupled with different management regimes being extremely popular for both public and private tenants in the UK and continental Europe. Management and maintenance issues are now seen as the preconditions in generating successful modern communities within high-rise estates. Evidence to support such arguments is still empirical with very little systematic research investigating the issues and themes for successful high living. Commercial tenant requirements are better understood and in a number of ways are easier to verify. Recent trends in workplace design, resulting from the use of modern IT technology shows a shift of preference towards larger floor-plates and plan shapes that allow seamless communication, mix of functions and flexibility for frequent expansion or contraction of operations. Simultaneously, branding is also shifting from the "exterior look" of the building (signature tenant occupier buildings like Swiss Re) to the "interior feel" (such as Google), which is more attuned to accommodating the high value knowledge worker. With a demanding and flexible corporate culture, tall individual office buildings refer more and more to a very specific clientele (financial sectors and more traditional service industry sectors) and do not reflect in any way the organisational needs of modern industries.

London's planning policy

The complexity issues and the difficulties of accumulating comprehensive data, makes deriving policy consensus across European cities, at best difficult and at worst futile. Metropolises such as Paris and London have taken

fig. 5a

fig. 5b

diametrically different approaches. Paris decided in the 1980s on a conservationist policy with the retention of a consistent morphology across the city centre. Renewal has been driven by intensification and adaptive reuse of established building envelopes, with any expansions confined to specific locations supported by comprehensive plans such as La Défense, Rive Gauche, etc. →fig. 5a,b At the same time London, a capital city of a similar scale, addresses the same issues in a very different way. Plan-

fig. 6a **Distinctiveness of London's skyline.
London, St Paul's from Westminster
Bridge, 2009**
fig. 6b **Distinctiveness of London's skyline.
London, St Paul's from Vauxhall
Bridge, 2005**
fig. 6c **Distinctiveness of London's skyline.
Photomontage of current at
the time planning applications
for tall buildings**

ning policy avoids a restrictive building height regulation at both local authority and strategic level decided by the Greater London Authority (GLA). The diversity of building heights and the inconsistencies in the skyline is regarded as being a dynamic expression of the city's economy and cultural base. The City of London in particular has traditionally relied on continuous renewal of its building stock driven by speculative development and a "negotiation" based planning system which shaped (relatively successfully so far) its physical character, with its medieval street plans as the constant. A key question for the City, also the issue that is considered the counterargument, is how long the city's silhouette will be recognised as uniquely London and not an average Far East city. →**fig. 6a,b,c**

The intrinsically different characters of these urban transformations are reflected in the respective planning systems. Paris relies on prescriptive zoning regulating or pre-designing the scale and grain of existing and

fig. 6a

fig. 6b

new places. London, on the other hand, continues to rely on very loose land-use/zoning plans and on a variety of guidance frameworks of a different level of specificity or prescriptiveness according to policy objectives and political preferences and so forth established at the time of publication. Exceptions are the larger, often single ownership projects such as Canary Warf, which are masterplans and even then are often extensively revised and repositioned along the way. Up until the mid-1990s planning policy in London was a result of the pattern generated by the policies of the 32 London Boroughs, but a more coordinated approach was established by the London Plan prepared and issued by the GLA (Greater London Authority) in 2004. Strategic advice on tall buildings is still generic and sets out the criteria and principles for consideration, which need to be taken on board by local authorities, but does not set specific preferred locations. A comparison of language usage in the Tall Building Planning Guidance of the 2004 policy plan and the draft replacement plan of 2009, indicates how political the issue is in the UK context. Subtleties in wording reflect clearly the "for" and "against" attitudes of respective Mayors and the intrinsic flexibility of interpretation the plan wants to retain.

The shape of London's skyline, despite strategic policy, continues to rely on individual local authorities' plans and development control processes for "case by case" approvals. All London Boroughs were required to review their tall building policies within their own administra-

fig. 6c

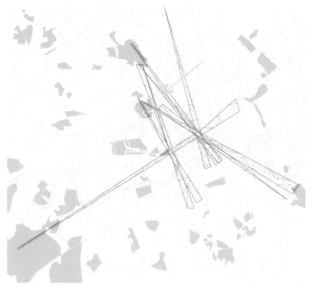

fig. 7

tive boundaries and act in accordance with the advice of the London Plan, but no consideration was given to plans in adjacent boroughs. Since the London Plan does not take a position on planning an overall geographical distribution of height, there are no planning tools to control the shape the city's skyline. Similarly the London Strategic Views framework, as the statutory-overriding framework, refers primarily to the central London area and expresses a key concern for safeguarding the views

London River Prospects:
A Tower Bridge, City Hall
B London Bridge
C Southwark Bridge
D Millennium Bridge
E Blackfriars Bridge
F Waterloo Bridge
G South Bank
H Hungerford Bridge
I Westminster Bridge
J Lambeth Bridge
K Victoria Embarkment
L Jubilee Gardens
M Albert Embankment

London Panoramas
Sightline to landmark Building
Public Place

Townscape Views:
1 Buckingham Palace from Mall
2 Palsce of Westminster from Hyde Park
3 Royal Naval College from Isle of Dogs
4 St. Jame's Park to Whitehall and Horse Guards

fig. 8a

towards St Paul's and other landmarks but not for the overall organisation of views. Such a remit is in principle limited and it is intrinsically incapable of comprehensively encompassing other considerations such as the impact of tall buildings on the underlying structure of the city, economic conditions, infrastructure, and local townscape with obvious implications. →fig. 7 Other considerations may be covered by other independent and uncoordinated policies.

The London Plan revised fundamentally the views framework in the mid-2000s and proposed a new Supplementary Planning Guidance (SPG). The London's View Management Framework shifts the emphasis from the protection of strategic views of the historic landmarks to the "management of the viewing experience" as a whole. It takes into account the compositional quality of the view and the experience of the viewer which may be static (studied) or sequential (glimpses as we move through a space). It defines an overall 26 viewing loca-

fig. 7   Impact of protected views from
            Kenwood on the local townscape
fig. 8a,b   London Views Management
            Framework

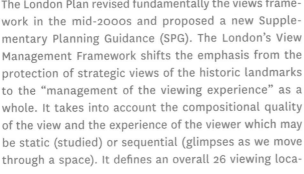

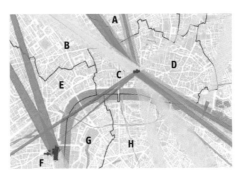

A Klington
B Camden
C st. Pauls Cathedral
D City of London
E City of Westminister
F Palace of Westminister
G Lambeth
H Soutwork

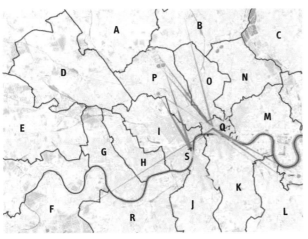

A Barnet
B Haringey
C Wetharm Forest
D Harrow
E Ealing
F Richmond Upon Thames
G Hamersmith and Fulhan
H Kennington and Chelsea
I City of Westminister
J Lambeth
K Southwork
L Lewisham
M Tower Hamlets
N Hackney
O Islington
P Camden
Q st. Pauls Cathedral
R Wandswarth
S Palace of Westminister

fig. 8b

View Object – skyline (background)

middle-ground

foreground

fig. 9a

fig. 9b

tions structured in 4 categories: the Panoramas (long distant views from beyond the central city), the Linear views (long axes within the central areas), River prospects (primarily across bridges), and Local townscape views (selective views near key landmarks). →fig. 8a,b Having suggested the settings, the framework goes further in setting up the generic aesthetic principles and some of the compositional quality of the experience of the viewer meaning that both the view itself and the position from which it is viewed are taken into consideration. It recognises that the foreground has an immediate and significant impact on the viewer's experience and the ambience of the viewing place itself. The middle ground, the link/area between foreground and background, holds also a primary significance in what is perceived as an aesthetic quality of the overall. →fig. 9a,b,c,d The background of the skyline configuration is distinctive as an overarching element with the backdrop as the compositional background to the object (or historic landmark).

While a new SPG suggests a more comprehensive and sophisticated views policy, it is difficult to see how the

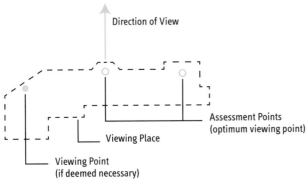

Direction of View

Assessment Points
(optimum viewing point)

Viewing Place

Viewing Point
(if deemed necessary)

fig. 9c

fig. 9a,b London Views Management Framework. View from Primrose Hill
fig. 9c,d Components of a protected vista

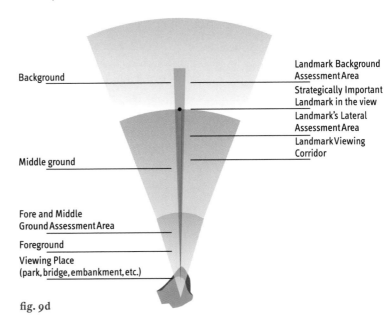

The Components of a Protected Vista

Background

Landmark Background
Assessment Area

Strategically Important
Landmark in the view

Landmark's Lateral
Assessment Area

Landmark Viewing
Corridor

Middle ground

Fore and Middle
Ground Assessment Area

Foreground

Viewing Place
(park, bridge, embankment, etc.)

fig. 9d

management of individual townscape settings (however successfully done) can result in an overall organised and predictable skyline configuration. It refers still to a local prescription of the shape of a skyline/townscape from geographically arbitrary points and with no way of taking into consideration the impact of the proposed skyline on the ground. This is in direct contrast to the way a zoning plan and density/height regulations normally organise city geographies, with the skyline being the result of such an organisation.

fig. 10 **New tall building typologies are more appropriate in the European context**

The role of architecture – a concluding note

The discipline of architecture continues to propose the same old-fashioned tall building type (central core narrow plan) with the innovation concentrating purely on the building form and shapes encouraged by the development of building technologies and engineering advances. Texture and association is also neglected despite significant development in construction and the use of new materials. Building aesthetics seems to be more and more generic and non-place specific, with a total lack of notional references to use, location, ownership or cultural context. It seems the central objective is their iconic and landmark value, often in direct competition with each other in vying for a unique image and market positioning.

If tall buildings are to become more relevant as part of the new morphological character of new city quarters, architects needs to review other typological aspects of building form and plan. →fig. 10 New typologies need to challenge the conservative and relatively old fashioned "slim" tall tower in favour of more diverse and versatile building forms. At the same time, the exploration of tall buildings in their context can suggest new morphologies and more thematic approaches to the evolution of the "European Tall Building". This may produce a more effective and perhaps developmentally familiar townscape.

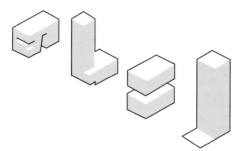

fig. 10

REFERENCES

— DEGW August 2002, London's Skyline, Views and High
Buildings, report for the Greater London Authority
(GLA),SDS Technical Report Nineteen (attached to the
London Plan)
— DEGW (1998) Rotterdam Municipality (Urbanism Unit),
High-rise Study
— DEGW (2000) Dublin High Building Strategy, Manage
Intensification and Change, Dublin Corporation.
— Colin Buchanan: The economic impact of high density
development and tall buildings in central business districts
for the British Property Federation, September 2008
— GLA 2009. Draft Revised Supplementary Planning
Guidance: London View Management Framework.
— MVRDV 1998. FARMAX excursions on Density,
010 publishers

IMAGE SOURCES

— {fig. 2} DEGW (2005)
— {fig. 3} MVRDV (1998), FARMAX excursions on Density,
010 publishers)
— {fig. 4} DEGW (1998) Rotterdam Municipality Urbanism
Unit, High rise Study
— {fig. 8} Source: Supplementary Planning Guidance, London
Views Management Framework (2007)
— {fig. 9} Source: Supplementary Planning Guidance, London
Views Management Framework (2007)
— {fig. 10} Source: Montevetro, Barrow Street Building,
concept design, Dublin 2007.

fig. 1 What is high?

4
Citius, Altius, Fortius.
Myths about High-rise

Daan Zandbelt

High-rise is often portrayed as the most effective instrument for the densification of our cities and the best way to keep a city compact. It is high time for a critical look at this notion.[1]

In late 2004, when the Taipei 101 tower opened in Taiwan, it was the world's tallest building, at 500 meters. It overshadowed the Petronas Towers in Kuala Lumpur (452 m) and the Sears Tower in Chicago (442 m). Only six towers were taller than 400 meters. That remained so until 2010, when the Burj Khalifa was completed. For a long time, its exact height was a secret. But now we know that, at 828 meters, the Burj dwarfs all other skyscrapers. How high is "high" anyway? →fig. 1

The world's forty largest skylines include only one in the European Union, in Paris. With 112 buildings over ninety meters high, Rotterdam is the only Dutch city in the European top ten, in fifth place, trailing Benidorm. That says enough. By international standards, the towers on Rotterdam's Wilhelminapier, which include the three tallest in the Netherlands, are not so much "high-rises" as "mid-rises". →fig. 2

---

[1] This article is based on research carried out by Zandbelt&vandenBerg for the Dutch Council on Tall Buildings (Stichting Hoogbouw). This research led to the publication of a book about high-rise culture in the Netherlands, *Hoogbouw, een studie naar Nederlandse hoogbouwcultuur* (2008), which is available free of charge from the Council.

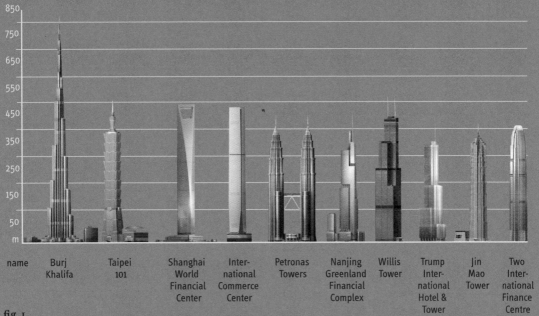

| name | Burj Khalifa | Taipei 101 | Shanghai World Financial Center | Inter-national Commerce Center | Petronas Towers | Nanjing Greenland Financial Complex | Willis Tower | Trump Inter-national Hotel & Tower | Jin Mao Tower | Two Inter-national Finance Centre |

fig. I

Even in the Netherlands, "high" is a relative term. Various legal standards govern what is defined as high. In buildings with five or more storeys, it is mandatory to install a lift. Above seventy meters, the national Buildings Decree *(Bouwbesluit)* requires special safety features such as a sprinkler system.

Furthermore, for about fifteen years now, almost every large municipality has had a policy or strategy on high-rise buildings that specifies how tall they can be and where they can be built. In The Hague, for instance, any building taller than fifty meters is considered a high-rise. In Utrecht and Zwolle, the boundary is thirty meters, and in Tilburg fifteen. Other standards are less abstract: no building may be higher than the Dom tower in Utrecht or, in Arnhem, exceed the height of the Veluwe Massif, or exceed the tree tops in Nijmegen and Wageningen – though apparently the trees in Nijmegen (at 25 m) are taller than those in Wageningen (at 18 m).

In short, "high-rise" – or, more fundamentally, "high" – is a relative term. One person's "low" is another person's "high", or even "too high". What is low in Rotterdam is

fig. 2 Higher is not necessarily more dense

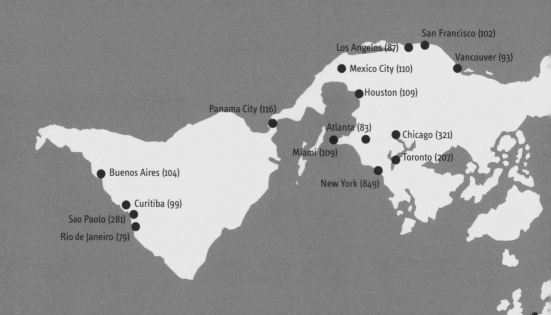

Honolulu (85)

San Francisco (102)

Los Angelos (87)

Vancouver (93)

Mexico City (110)

Houston (109)

Panama City (116)

Atlanta (83)

Chicago (321)

Miami (109)

Toronto (207)

Buenos Aires (104)

New York (849)

Curitiba (99)

Sao Paolo (281)

Rio de Janeiro (79)

Paris (112)

Top 10 of skylines European Union

City	Number>90m
1 Parijs	112
2 London	49
3 Frankfurt	38
4 Benidorm	35
5 Rotterdam	29
6 Brussel	22
7 Warschau	21
8 Wenen	20
9 Madrid	17
10 Berlin	15

Tokyo (572)
Osaka (124)
Seoul (273)
Shanghai (549)
Beijing (234)
Xiamen (82)
Manila (183)
Hong Kong (2939)
Wuhan (98)
Guangzhou (233)
Shenzhen (199)
Chongqing (232)
Jakarta (129)
Chengdu (94)
Singapore (296)
Bangkok (382)
Kuala Lumpur (215)
Moscow (150)
Mumbai (90)
Istanbul (94)
Dubai (268)
Sydney (138)
Melbourne (97)

Top 10 of skylines world-wide

City	Number>90m
1 Hongkong	2.939
2 New York	849
3 Tokyo	572
4 Shanghai	549
5 Bangkok	382
6 Chicago	321
7 Singapore	296
8 Sao Paulo	281
9 Seoul	273
10 Dubai	268

fig. 3 Same volume, same footprint but lower

0 | | | | | 50 m.

Rotterdam
Bergpolderflat

Footprint	ca. 600 m² (9 stories)
Site	ca. 4250 m²
FSI	1,3

high in Wageningen. And what is high in Rotterdam is low in Shanghai or Chicago. There are many myths and mis-understandings about high-rises. And that is quite apart from the tall stories (whose is biggest?), though admittedly, the theme is often "more, more, more". *Citius, altius, fortius.* Time to bust a few high-rise myths.

A densification machine?

High-rise construction is emblematic of high density. But all too often, the emblem is confused with the reality and high-rises are seen as the only way to achieve higher densities. For instance, the strategic plan for the Randstad in 2040 *(Structuurvisie Randstad 2040)*, developed under the Ministers Cramer, Eurlings, and Verburg, has fostered a belief that high-rises are the royal road to urban densification in the Randstad. "Because space is limited, housing must rise to new heights."[2] But height does not necessarily translate into density. →fig. 3

High towers often have flat feet. At ground level, a large, tall building requires many additional facilities, such as parking, pipes, cables, lobbies, and space for circula-

---

[2] Source: NOS broadcast, "Meer hoogbouw in de Randstad", Wednesday 18 November 2009.

Rotterdam
Perimeter block, Rotterdam Bergpolde

Footprint   ca. 3000 m² (5 stories)
Site   ca. 7500 m² (e.g. block
FSI   2,0

fig. 3

tion and distribution. Because what goes up must come down, the base of the building must be much larger than the tower (or slab) on top of it.

One illustration is the Bergpolderflat in Rotterdam's Oude Noorden district. This is the first gallery flat build-ing *(galerijflat)*, a Dutch housing type invented by Wil-lem van Tijen. The complex is in a pre-war district with perimeter blocks that are five storeys high. It towers over these surroundings, but takes up only a small part of the block. The block that includes the Bergpolderflat in fact has a lower Floor Space Index (a metric of den-sity) than the traditional perimeter blocks around it. There is a fairly large open space around the building, because of sunlight and wind issues.

This is characteristic of high-rises in general. Only true high-rise environments with many towers close to-gether, such as Chelsea in Manhattan, have a degree of density like that of pre-war cities. We do not have such environments in the Netherlands (at least, not yet).

In many other cases, high-rises have proved incapable of turning the dream of high density into a reality. Take the Montevideo building in Rotterdam, →fig. 4 which until recently was the tallest residential tower in the Nether-lands. This 152-meter tower rests on a base that takes up almost five times as much space as the tower itself. If

fig. 4 **Higher is more expensive too.**
        Montevideo Rotterdam
fig. 5 **Low finances high**

you lay down the tower on the low-rise base, you would have a much lower building with the same volume and the same footprint.

fig. 4

Money machine?

It is often thought that tall buildings make it possible to recoup high land prices. If this is true, then the skyline is a three-dimensional graph of land values: the tallest buildings stand on the most expensive plots. More construction is necessary to earn back the purchase price of the land, and therefore, the reasoning goes, taller buildings are a must.

But this argument doesn't hold water (at least, not in the Netherlands). Here, we work with land residual value, a complex technique. The long and short of it is that the price of the land (and municipal fees) are determined "in consultation", according to the cubic content of the structures to be developed, their purpose, and their value. The more you build, the more expensive the land is. This is certainly quite a baffling, and indeed nonsensical, system. Moreover, high-rise construction is more expensive than traditional low-rise methods. Dutch high-rises are often made financially feasible by combining them with low-rises. The profit from the low-rises subsidizes the tall tower. →fig. 5

A success story?

Tall buildings are large buildings, a fact which developers sometimes forget. This places severe limits on the
implementation and success of high-rise projects. The
view from the top is, of course, spectacular; those "meters" are the first to be sold, along with the base. The
middle of the building often remains vacant for quite a
while. Compared to low-rise developments, skyscrapers
are difficult to phase in: I have yet to see a tower built
in two stages. And the property developed is usually
rather homogeneous, with a single function and little typological diversity. The market is quickly saturated, and
it takes a long time before everything is sold or rented.
This places a heavy financial burden on the investor.

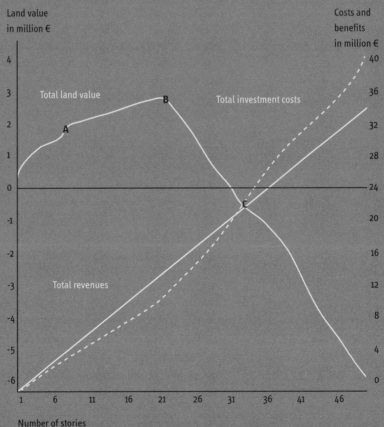

fig. 5   Revenues versus investment per dwelling in high-rises. Daalhuisen (2004)

fig. 6a High-rise does not equal urbanity

Mixed-use towers are hardly ever constructed in the Netherlands, because they are even more complex than single-use ones. This is because they require separate (and therefore more) lifts and involve complex ownership structures, etc. Rem Koolhaas's project on the Wilhelminapier, De Rotterdam, is the exception that proves the rule. It took twelve years before construction even began. And after completion, the three municipal office towers on the Marconiplein will become vacant, because all city officials are to move out of them and into the Wilhelminapier development. In other words, De Rotterdam depends on a major municipal commitment.

An urban icon?

Towers symbolize not only high density but also city life. This is why cities want high-rises; they are the icons of a self-respecting metropolis. Nevertheless, in medium-sized Dutch cities, tower blocks do not do well. For the same price, buyers can purchase detached or semi-detached houses, close to town, with large gardens and garages. Those who buy high-rise apartments are deliberately opting for an urban setting and lifestyle. They expect a range of exceptional restaurants, interesting festivals, special boutiques, services and facilities. But medium-sized cities simply don't offer all that.

fig. 6a

Quality is the key

All the traditional, supposedly iron-clad arguments for high-rises in the Netherlands do not hold up under scrutiny. Greater height does not necessarily mean greater density or more urban character. These buildings do not even make a lot of money, let alone meet a major demand.

This is not to say that high-rises should never be built. On the contrary, they should be built, but for the right reasons. Subjective criteria, questions of taste, are what matter most.

Towers can be beautiful, provide fantastic views, keep major employers from relocating, symbolize a new stage in urban development, or enhance the legibility or cohesion of the city as a whole. In any event, tall buildings are striking buildings. They can be seen from far away and attract a great deal of attention. This is all the more reason to invest in quality. If it is clear that the budget will not permit an especially impressive building, why bother? Mediocre tower blocks for seniors on the outskirts of the city – where is the good in that? Put it out of your mind and set your sights lower. In the compact city, high-rises are an opportunity, not a necessity. →fig. 6a,b

IMAGE SOURCES
All images by Zandbelt&vandenBerg

Panoramic view with urban facilities nearby..

.. or your own garage and garden?

fig. 1 **Urban density and transport-related energy consumption**

5
Sustainable
Urban Form

Meta Berghauser Pont[1]

ABSTRACT The search for more sustainable urban patterns is at the core of this article. Often, this discussion does not go further than a discussion concerning compact cities versus sprawl. Starting from the importance of higher densities, this article explores the subject of density in relation to urban form much deeper by looking into a variety of performances. Issues that will be discussed are, amongst others, the role of density in terms of daylight access, urbanity (or urban vitality) and CO_2 emissions. We will see that performances often contradict each other and finding the most sustainable solutions is a question of optimizing all of them simultaneously. The Spacematrix method (Berghauser Pont and Haupt 2010) will be used as a starting point to do so.

Compact cities versus sprawl

Most past and present discussions on the sustainability of urban patterns concern the pros and cons of compact cities versus sprawl. There is among many researchers and professionals a consensus that compact high density settlements are more sustainable than low density

[1] This paper is based on the lecture given by Meta Berghauser Pont during the sLIM series on April 16, 2010 in Rotterdam. With special thanks to Per Haupt who has written the book *Spacematrix. Space, Density and Urban Form* together with me. Parts of this paper are based on this book and other work done together.

sprawl, and that – in light of the rapid growth of meg-
alopolises – dense cities will somehow halt an unsustainable increase of consumption of transport, energy
and resources. Newman and Kenworthy (1999) demonstrated that in low-density cities in North America energy consumption per inhabitant for transport is far
higher than the same energy used by Europeans, and
even more so when compared to very high-density cities
in Japan. North Americans are almost totally dependent
on the private car, while the Japanese in general cluster
in higher densities and are able to sustain a more efficient public transport network. →fig. 1

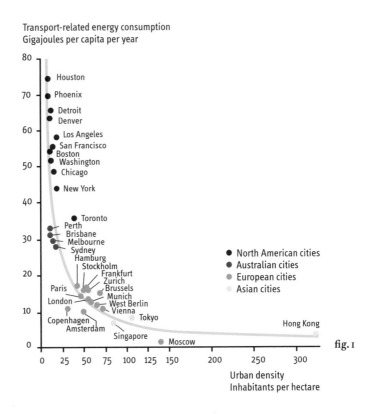

fig. 1

European cities do well in this respect. However, the increase in individual housing allocations, the functional
zoning of cities into separate areas for housing, green
space (for example parks, graveyards and sports fields),
offices and industries, and the increased use of the car
(wider streets with more parking facilities) have since
around 1900 all contributed to an increased urban footprint. In a city like Amsterdam, the urban footprint has

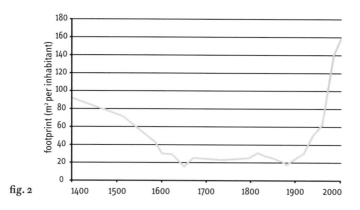

fig. 2

been exponentially increasing since the end of the 19th century. The annual growth of the urban footprint in Amsterdam is 1.9 per cent. →fig. 2 Expressed another way, one could say that every new generation in Amsterdam since 1900 has had the double amount of urban space at its disposal – or lives half as densely – as their parents. If industrialization took off with urbanization and over-crowding in the 19th century, the fossil-fuel-driven economic growth, driven by developments in transport techniques of the last century, have dispersed and thinned out many of our cities. →fig. 3

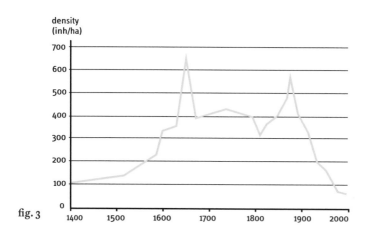

fig. 3

Thus, although European cities are rather dense in comparison to their American counterparts, all European cities have thinned out dramatically over the last 100 years. Another development, intimately related to the rapid increase of the urban footprint, concerns the increased fossil fuel consumption and greenhouse gas emissions.

After a stable value of less than 280 ppm of carbon dioxide equivalents in the atmosphere before 1950, the world is currently approaching the value of 400 ppm. Based on observations by Goddard Institute for Space Studies (GISS), we live today in a world that is on average almost one degree Celsius warmer than before industrialization took off. →fig. 4 If we want this increase to halt at two degrees Celsius above pre-industrial levels, which by the scientific community is deemed a dangerous tipping point, CO_2 has to stabilize at approximately 450 ppm, often described as the red line. The IPCC models indicate that if we are to stay on the "safe" side of this red line, many industrialized countries will have to quickly reduce emissions by 80–90%. It thus becomes important for planners and designers to get a grip on the magnitude of necessary transitions needed to halt the concentration of greenhouse gases responsible for climate change. How we use space constitutes a large chunk of our present predicaments, and as transport and buildings are responsible for some two thirds of CO_2 emissions in rich countries (Neale 2008), much can be gained by organizing urban space differently.

fig. 2 Urban footprint for the city of
       Amsterdam from 1400 to 2000
fig. 3 Density developments in the city of
       Amsterdam from 1400 to 2000
fig. 4 Global temperature change from 1880
       until 2010

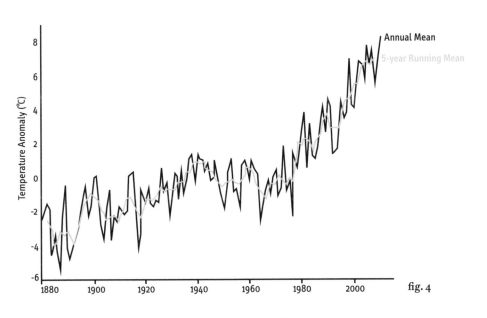

fig. 4

fig. 5a

fig. 5b

The transition towards higher densities

Higher densities are one of the solutions for achieving more sustainable cities. Not only does this have a positive effect on the use of public transport, it also contributes to more vibrant urban areas. The concept of vitality or urbanity is frequently used to describe a human condition of plurality, difference, interaction and communication (Hajer 1989, Heeling *et al.* 2002, Jacobs 1961, Lozano 2007, Urhahn 1996, Van der Wouden 1999, Zijderveld 1983). Although all kinds of social and spatial factors are involved in producing diversity, a dense concentration of people is one of the prerequisites for a flourishing and diverse city: "The other factors that influence how much diversity is generated, and where, will have nothing much to influence if enough people are not there." (Jacobs 1992, p. 205)

Two fundamentally different approaches to achieving higher densities have dominated practice during the last century. Le Corbusier and Gropius, amongst others, argued that by planning for higher buildings, one could provide more open space without losing out on the number of dwellings and population density (Rådberg 1988). Christopher Alexander (1977), arguing against the Modernist high-rise developments, introduced psychological arguments to subject all buildings to height restrictions. Jane Jacobs who saw low densities as a threat to the liveliness of cities, but blamed high-rise for robbing the city of its vitality, believed in compact urban patterns with high densities (Jacobs 1992, p. 214). This would bring people out into the public streets and parks, and create a lively city. Jan Gehl recently used the same argument for a high degree of coverage and density in his study for Ørestad Syd in Copenhagen (Christiansen 2006).

Let's try to understand the differences between these two approaches by comparing two urban areas: Märkisches Viertel in Berlin and Grachtengordel in Amsterdam. The first is composed of high-rise slabs of approximately 14 storeys built in the 1960s, and the second is composed of perimeter building blocks of around four storeys built in the 17th century. Both with the same, and for the European context, relative high FSI (or FAR). →fig. 5a,b

By looking at the two examples we can conclude that land use intensity (FSI or FAR) does not allow us to differentiate between them in spatial terms. In this article we will therefore use the Spacematrix method (Berghauser Pont and Haupt 2010) which combines three density measures to be able to differentiate between various urban patterns such as spacious versus compact developments with similar high densities. In order to simultaneously assess these, a three-dimensional diagram has been constructed. The Spacematrix: FSI on the z-axis expresses the built intensity of a certain area, GSI on the x-axis is an indicator of the compactness of the built

fig. 5a Märkisches Viertel in Berlin
fig. 5b Grachtengordel in Amsterdam

environment, and N on the y-axis describes the network density, and is as such an indicator of the size of the urban layout. →**fig. 6**

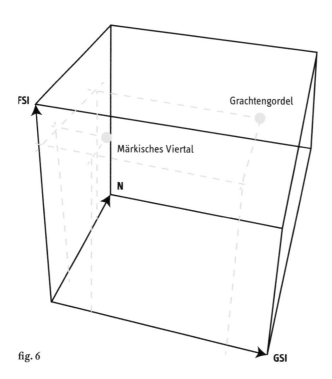

fig. 6

The variables of Spacematrix are defined and calculated as follows (at urban fabric level and thus including public streets; for more details see Berghasuer Pont and Haupt 2010):

1. Floor Space Index (FSI) is calculated as follows:
$$FSI= F/Af$$
Where F is gross floor area in m², and Af is the area of the urban fabric in m².

2. Ground Space Index (GSI) is calculated as follows:
$$GSI=B/Af$$
Where B is the built up surface or building footprint in m², and Af is the area of the urban fabric in m².

3. Network density (N) is calculated as follows:
$$Nf=(\Sigma li+(\Sigma le)/2)/Af$$
Where li is the metrical length of the internal network (within the fabric), le is the metrical length of the exter-

nal network (corresponding to the boundaries of the urban fabric), and Af is the area of the urban fabric in m².

fig. 6 Two samples in Spacematrix with floor space index (FSI) on the y-axis, ground space index (GSI) on the x-axis, and network density (N) on the z-axis

If the two examples, Märkisches Viertel and Grachtengordel, mentioned earlier are positioned in the Spacematrix we can see that not only spatially, but also quantitatively they differ greatly from one another. Märkisches Viertel combines a relatively high FSI (1.81) with a low GSI (0.13). Grachtengordel has a similar FSI (1.94), but has a much higher GSI (0.48). The network densities of the two samples are rather different too. Märkisches Viertel has a network density of 0.005 while Grachtengordel has a network density of 0.012. →fig. 5

Further, other indicators can be calculated based on these three main variables FSI, GSI and N such as OSR which expresses the pressure on the unbuilt land, L that indicates the average building height in the area, and the grain of the urban layout (w). These measures are calculated as follows:

4. Open Space Index (OSR) is calculated as follows:
$$OSR_f=(1-GSI_f)/FSI_f$$

5. Average building height (L) is calculated as follows:
$$L=FSI_f/GSI_f$$

6. Mesh size (w) is calculated as follows:
$$w=2/N$$

Märkisches Viertel has, due to the high FSI and low GSI, a relatively high OSR (0.48). In other words, for every 100 m² of floor space, 48 m² of open space is available in the urban fabric. Grachtengordel combines almost the same FSI (1.94) with a high GSI (0.48) and thus a lower OSR (0.27). Here, 100 m² of floor space is compensated for only 27 m² open space. Hoenig was the first to systematically study spaciousness (OSR) in relation to density and in his article "Baudichte und Weiträumigkeit", he used it as a measurement of the quality of an urban plan, regarding more green per m² of floor space as positive (Rådberg 1988, Hoenig 1928). In his view an OSR should be at least 1.00 and even Märkisches Viertel was thus regarded as too crowded. The average height and mesh size of the urban layout of the two examples is

fig. 7a Märkisches Viertel in Berlin
fig. 7b Grachtengordel in Amsterdam

4.1 resp. 164 m for Grachtengordel and 14.0 resp. 394 m for Märkisches Viertel. In other words, the buildings of Märkisches Viertel are more than three times higher than those in Grachtengordel and the urban blocks in the Grachtengordel are nearly three times smaller than those in Märkisches Viertel. →fig. 7a,b

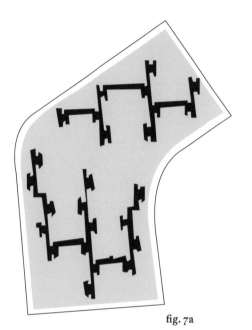

fig. 7a

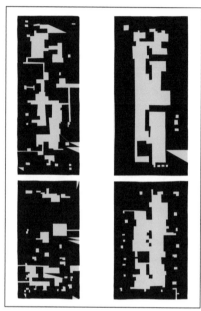

fig. 7b

The performance of high-rise and spacious versus low-rise but compact densities

Density plays a role in this as we have discussed earlier, but also block size (grain of the urban layout) is crucial to the vitality of urban places. In other words, vitality and diversity flourish in the upper-right-far-back area in the Spacematrix diagram. But of course there are many more properties involved in the discussion surrounding the notion of urbanity. Without taking a stance on any correct definition, urbanity is delineated here into separate sub-properties, focusing on the physical-spatial aspects of the built environment. We suggest that physical factors such as interface (the relationship between buildings and network), building surface (coverage), grain (or block) size, profile width and tare space (proportion of private and public space) can be viewed as elements contributing to a description and understanding of the concept of urbanity. Three indicators, all derived from the Spacematrix measures, will be discussed here: Network Space Ratio (NSR) as an indicator of the user intensity of public space, Exposure Ratio (ER) as an indicator of commercial vitality and Connectivity Ratio (CR) as an indicator of the variety of routes to choose from going from A to B (Berghauser Pont and Haupt 2010).

With the Network Space Ratio (NSR), the OSR of the public space can be captured. A high coverage on the scale of the island, combined with high built intensity (FSI) and little network (tare) space on fabric level, generates a high intensity of movements and interaction between people in the streets (or other public open space). NSR is calculated as follows:

$$7. \; NSRf = \Delta OSR = OSRf\text{-}OSRi$$

If NSR is considered in isolation, more programme on larger islands increases the "pressure" on the public network. However, the network density (N) decreases which is considered less optimal for city diversity. Further, the exposure (or accessibility) of the islands itself decreases. The potential exposure of private space (islands) in relation to public (network) space depends on the measurements of the islands alone. Large islands have relatively little exposure (or accessibility) as the potential façade length is limited. This Exposure Ratio (ER) can be formulated as the potential façade length to island area. The potential façade length is thus equivalent to the length of the perimeter of the island. ER is calculated as follows:

$$8. \; ERi = (Ai*GSIi)/pi$$
Where pi is the perimeter of the island in m.

The number of intersections as an indicator for circulation convenience is considered to be another important factor in relation to urbanity (Siksna 1997). The (internal) connectivity of a fabric can be said to be conditioned by this factor (Marshall 2005). In fabrics with more streets and intersections (and thus smaller islands), people have a larger variety of routes to choose from. This stimulates interaction which is seen as one defining characteristic of urbanity. Both island size and the numbers of crossings are related to network density (N). The Connectivity Ratio (CR), or the amount of crossings per hectare, increases proportionally to the square of the network density. CR is thus calculated as follows:

$$9. \ CRf = N2/4$$

An interesting observation that can be made from the above analysis of the basic geometry of the fabric (and its relation to properties that are often considered to be central to urbanity), is the conflicting nature of the pressure on public space (NSR), the exposure of the islands (ER) and (internal) connectivity (CR). All are regarded as important to urbanity. Intensity is (internally) generated not only by the amount of programme and its primary distribution, but also by the amount of network that has to accommodate the generated movements. Less network, and thus larger islands, concentrates the movements and thus increases the user intensity of the network. However, this increase of scale conflicts with and is tempered by the architectural organization of the island. The exposure and accessibility of the island and the human scale of a walkable urban fabric put a limit on the simplistic endeavour for a higher user intensity in public space. The tension between these performances produces an outcome that is a compromise, neither too large nor too small.

The energy consumption for mobility, and connected to that CO_2 emissions, is another performance that is related directly to density as Newman and Kenworthy (1999) have shown. Pre-industrial, dense city settlements provided (and still do) a relatively large catchment area, even when most movements are made on foot. The developments in transport techniques, and related to this the sprawling of our cities, increased this catchment. A half-hour trip by foot, bike or car approximately covers an area of 20, 175 and 700 km² respectively. For equal densities (FSI and N) one could roughly state that the car has increased the potential for employment, commercial spending and social contact by more than 35 times compared to the most ancient transport method and four times compared to the bike. However, if a high-density city layout (the inner city of Amsterdam, for instance, with an FSI of 2.0) with walking and biking as dominant modalities is compared to a layout with low densities relying mainly on transport by car (for instance Phoenix, Arizona, FSI 0.1), and the catchment is expressed in floor area and not in ground surface only, then the advantage of potential interaction for the car decreases to a factor of almost two compared to walking. Here, network density is not even taken into consideration. If we assume that the grain of the urban layout is much finer in Amsterdam in comparison to Phoenix, one could reach more floor space by walking in Amsterdam than one could by driving through Phoenix. But even without taking the street pattern into account, the bike in Amsterdam performs better than the car in Phoenix: five times as much floor space is within the reach of the biker compared to the motorist. If public transport options such as tram, bus and metro are considered, public transport scores between four (tram and bus) and twelve (metro) times better than the private car (potential floor area that can be reached). Low-density, car-dependent layouts provide less choice (less potential floor area, or activity, to interact with), while consuming more energy and producing more CO_2 compared to higher densities with public transport.

Conclusions on sustainable densities

Taking into account all these different aspects of sustainability and its relation to density, we can conclude that the rather simple question "What is the most sustainable density?" does not have a simple answer. High-rise solutions with a relatively high density such as Märkische Viertel, perform well in terms of daylight access, access to open space (OSR) and the pressure on the network is relatively high (NSR). This means that daylight enters the interior of the buildings easily and also the open space surrounding these have sufficient daylight access. It also means that despite the intensity of the built up area, people have quite a lot of open space to use for playing, relaxing, and maybe more importantly, for the opportunity to start growing vegetables in an urban setting. Furthermore, the street space is used in an efficient way as movement is concentrated. However, high-rise solutions such as Märkische Viertel score much lower when look-

fig. 8 **Composite of compact high-rise and low-rise (Hong Kong)**

ing at the exposure ratio (ER) and the connectivity ratio (CR). In other words, the large islands provide little opportunity for exposure. This means that commercial and public uses have diminished potential in terms of finding good locations. Furthermore, the street layout gives people a small variety of routes to choose from when going from A to B. Grachtengordel performs better in that respect, but the pressure on the network and the daylight performance is lower. Both can be optimized by working on all performances simultaneously. The result might be a composite of high-rise and low-rise. →fig. 8

However, denser urban environments with an optimal balance of all performances do not automatically mean less transport and energy consumption. Distances between homes and places of work, regulations and fiscal policies probably have far greater impacts on car use than the mere physical layout of cities and regions (Neuman 2005). If the argument is turned around, though, one has to admit that dense settlements are a necessary prerequisite if we are to aspire to a radical reduction in car and lorry transportation. Only dense settlements offer feasible circumstances for the large investments needed for a more energy-efficient and environmentally responsible movement of goods and people. We can thus only discuss the potential sustainability of urban patterns which can then be actualized when it is matched by an organisation of human life that exploits this potential. Spacematrix can be helpful in finding the best spatial solutions taking into account a variety of performances. Here only a few have been discussed. Further research should be done to involve even more performances and be able to make informed decisions on sustainable urban form.

REFERENCES

— Alexander, C., et al. (1977). *A Pattern Language: Towns, Buildings, Construction.* New York: Oxford University Press, pp. 114–119.
— Berghauser Pont, M. Y., Haupt, P (2010), SPACEMATRIX, Space, Density and Urban Form. Rotterdam, NAi Publishers.
— Christiansen, J. (2006), Presentation of Jan Gehl's studies by Jan Christiansen, city architect of Copenhagen, at the

fig. 8

conference Scale, Form and Process. Scales in Urban Landscapes, Aarhus School of Architecture, Department of Landscape and Urbanism, Aarhus, Denmark, 23–24 February 2006.

— Hajer, M. (1989), De stad als publiek domein, Amsterdam: Wiardi Beckman Stichting.

— Heeling, J., H. Meyer and J. Westrik, (2002), Het ontwerp van de stadsplattegrond, Amsterdam: SUN.

— Hoenig, A. (1928), "Baudichte und Weitraumigkeit", Baugilde 10, p. 713–715.

— Jacobs, J. (1992, originally published in 1961), The Death and Life of Great American Cities, New York: Random House.

— Lozano, E. (2007), "Density in Communities, or the Most Important Factor in Building Urbanity", in: M. Larice and E. Macdonald (eds.), The Urban Design Reader, Oxon: Routledge, p. 312–327.

— Marshall, S. (2005), Streets & Patterns, Oxon: Spon Press.

— Meyer, H., F. de Josselin de Jong and M.J. Hoekstra (eds.) (2006), Het ontwerp van de openbare ruimte. Amsterdam: SUN, p. 9–30.

— Neale, J. (2008), Stop Global Warming, Cambridge: Bookmarks Publications, p. 71.

— Neuman, M. (2005), "The Compact City Fallacy", Journal of Planning Education and Research 25, 11–26.

— Newman, P. and J. Kenworthy (1999), Sustainability and Cities: Overcoming Automobile Dependence, Chicago: University of Chicago Press.

— Punter, J. (2007), Design guidelines in American cities: conclusions. In: M. Larice & E. Macdonald, eds. 2007. The urban design reader. Oxon: Routledge. pp. 500–516. Original text from 1997.

— Rådberg, J. (1988), Doktrin och täthet i svenskt stadsbyggande 1875–1975. Stockholm: Statens råd för byggnadsforskning.

— Saunders, W.S. (2006), Cappuccino urbanism, and beyond. Harvard Design Magazine, fall 2006/winter 2007, p. 3.

— Siksna, A. (1997), "The Effects of Block Size and Form in North American and Australian City Centres", Urban Morphology 1, 19–33.

— Urhahn, G.B. and M. Bobic (1996), Strategie voor stedelijkheid, Bussum: Uitgeverij THOTH.

— Wouden, R. van der (ed.) (1999) De stad op straat: De openbare ruimte in perspectief, The Hague: Sociaal en Cultureel Planbureau.

— Zijderveld, A.C. (1983), Steden zonder stedelijkheid:
Cultuurhistorische verkenning van een beleidsprobleem,
Deventer: van Loghum Slaterus.
IMAGE SOURCES

— {fig. 1} UNEP (2008). Urban density and transport-related
energy consumption. In UNEP/GRID-Arendal Maps and
Graphics Library (http://maps.grida.no/go/graphic/
urban-density-and-transport-related-energy-consumption)
— {fig. 2} Berghauser Pont and Haupt (2010)
— {fig. 3} Berghauser Pont and Haupt (2010)
— {fig. 4} Hansen, J.E., R. Ruedy, Mki. Sato, M. Imhoff, W.
Lawrence, D. Easterling, T. Peterson, and T. Karl, 2001: A
closer look at United States and global surface tempera-
ture change. J. Geophys. Res., 106, 23947-23963,
doi:10.1029/2001JD000354
— {fig. 5} Märkische Viertel: Berghauser Pont and Haupt (2010);
Grachtengordel: Berghauser Pont and Haupt(2005),
The Spacemate: Density and the Typomorphology of the
urban Fabric, in: Nordic Journal of Architectural Research,
2005/4, pp. 55–68
— {fig. 6} Based on image published in Berghauser Pont
and Haupt (2010)
— {fig. 7} Berghauser Pont and Haupt (2010)
— {fig. 8} Photo by author

fig. 1 Street and building

6
High-rise and Rotterdam

Emiel Arends

In the late 1990s, the City of Rotterdam initiated a high-rise vision in collaboration with urban planners DEGW. At that time high-rises were recognized as tools for densification and mixed use in the inner city. They also gave expression to the modernity of the city and further developed the skyline. The vision was implemented by amending existing land-use plans. High-rise zoning as outlined in the Inner City Plan of 1993 had not been clearly defined and, by the first revision, had already acquired multiple meanings. With an increasing supply of high-rise buildings a number of things had become clear.

On the basis of this vision, the number of solitary skyscrapers (stand alones) increased sharply, and were usually accompanied by an unattractive environment around the buildings. However, in order to achieve a continuous urban fabric, it is important to focus attention on the form and scale of city blocks and facades, and basically everything that surrounds the high-rises.

Some parts of the inner city high-rise zone had no stipulated limits on building heights. The concept of "the sky is the limit" has however delivered a lot of towers of uniform height rather than a few special highpoints. Each subsequent generation of high-rise buildings was higher than the previous one, but the result is that there is no real diversification in the skyline nor a highpoint, like traditionally a church tower might have been.

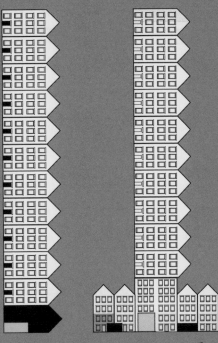
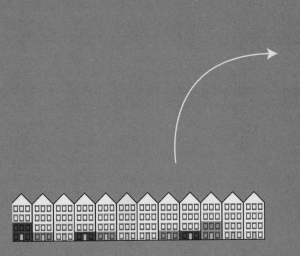

fig. I

Furthermore, a few questions have been raised concerning the volume of high-rises in combination with the size of their plot. A very high FSI causes many problems on the ground floor of buildings. The essential utilities and services required for a high-rise to function →fig. I need to be organised at ground level, so a high density plot means more space is needed in the plinth. A programme of densification should mean that the building is also giving something back to the city, but this is seldom the case. Blind street level facades, gaping holes or gates for parking garage entrances, messy facilities and container areas, etc. – all the things necessary to the proper functioning of a high-rise – are tending to dominate our urban street views and experiences.

Apart from the look and size of high-rise buildings, there are also significant side-effects concerning wind and shade. The high-rise vision had to be implemented within the boundaries of the existing land-use plans, meaning that the design requirements regulating the effects of wind and shade were also governed by the different criteria per location.

The concerns raised led to a review of Rotterdam's high-rise policy. The 2008 Inner City Plan already underlined not so much the importance of the role of high-rise, but the way high-rise should contribute to the city. The plan's central theme was the "city centre as the city's

fig. 2 High-rises need to contribute
        to the city lounge
fig. 3 Rotterdam high-rise zone

lounge", with the objective of developing the inner city as a vibrant, high quality meeting place. Accommodation and entertainment were to make a vital contribution to Rotterdam's quality of life. For high-rises this meant that their street level would have to be an essential part of Rotterdam's street life. →fig.2

While the first high-rise vision looked at the city as a whole, the 2010 revision focused on the inner city of Rotterdam. The main high-rise axis (Weena Coolsingel, Schiedamsedijk, Wilhelminaplein) combined with various concentrations of high-rises (such as Wilhelminapier and Wijnhaveneiland) are not in question and form the accepted foundation of the revision. The issues are not about overall image and skyline, but rather the picture at street level and how skyscrapers can participate in the desired "city lounge" experience. →fig.3

Re-examining the issues proved once again that knowledge and definitions of high-rise are not fixed and that there are many different definitions for the same things. It also made clear that too much of the focus had been on city image and the high-rise as a landmark, rather than the implications of high-rise at street level. In order

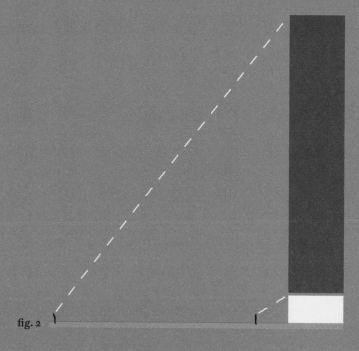

fig. 2

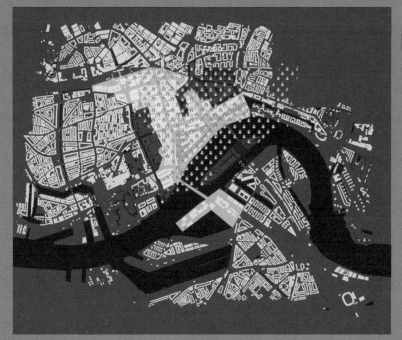

Hoogbouw zone

Hoogbouw zone

Hoogbouw zone ontzien

fig. 3

to get a better understanding of the issues, Rotterdam contracted expertise from various disciplines dealing with high-rise. A comprehensive study into the existing stock of high-rises was also carried out, looking specifically at their impact on the street. Comparisons of the situation in Rotterdam with high-rise buildings in Asia, America and the Middle East were meaningless. The inner city's post-war reconstruction plan by Van Traa (1946) used smaller and narrower block sizes than in foreign cities. This pattern and urban design of the inner city of Rotterdam determines (and limits) to a large extent the possible use of high-rises. →fig.4

With the primary focus of the high-rise revision being the way that a tower is experienced – particularly at street level – it became evident that high-rises should be more a part of the urban layer of the inner city. This is the layer most experienced by pedestrians. This means that in the future new high-rises should follow the building line of a street or square. There should also be more room in the lower part of a high-rise to avoid the utilitarian parts defining the appearance. More transparency and (semi) public functions are required. The vision

fig. 4 Street alignment and high-rise
fig. 5 High-rise and functions
fig. 6 Slenderness principles

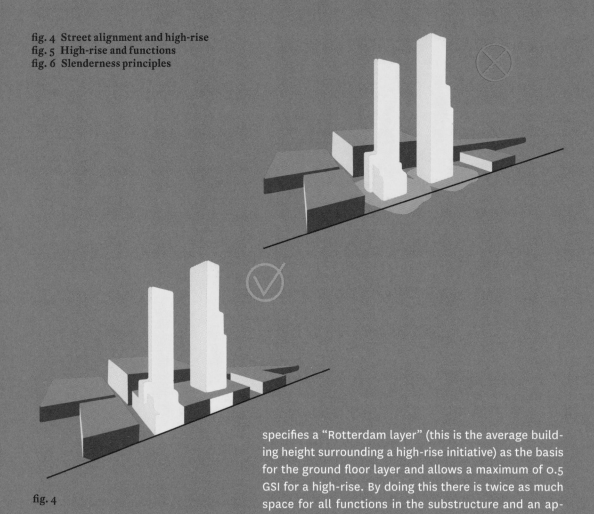

fig. 4

specifies a "Rotterdam layer" (this is the average building height surrounding a high-rise initiative) as the basis
for the ground floor layer and allows a maximum of 0.5
GSI for a high-rise. By doing this there is twice as much
space for all functions in the substructure and an appropriate amount of space for the most public functions
at street level while also reducing utilitarian logistics
there.

High-rises in the inner city now have a theoretical limit
of 200 meters along the main axis. This height will increase over time, but ensures that the latest generation of high-rises can still be built – those between 150
and 200 meters, which have turned out to be the most
economically feasible in Rotterdam. While the aim is to
create a gradual growth of the skyline, the new 200 meter limit also has an economic reason. By restricting the
height, a plot with an over-full program (to recover investment costs) is avoided. →fig.5

There are regulations to maximize floor space in order
to avoid excessive programs on a single plot in addition

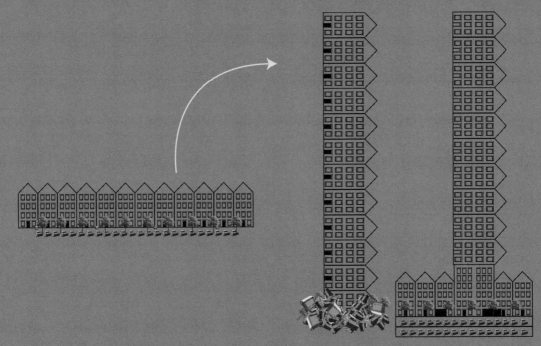

fig. 5

to the 0.5 GSI. For a high-rise up to 70 meters, a diagonal in the floor plan of maximum 56 meters is allowed
(equivalent to a floor space of 1600 m² and 40×40 m).
This size corresponds to the largest floor area for offices.
Above 70 meters the maximum diagonal is 42 meters
(equivalent to a floor area of 900 m² or 30×30 m). The
size corresponds to the largest floor areas for residential towers. Some plots in the city are much larger and
incorporate enough space to allocate the utilities appro-
priately within the given space. For these plots (larger
than 3200 m²), the rules regarding the diagonals do not
apply. →fig.6

The problem of shadows cast by high-rises has been
compensated by allocating various "sun spots". →fig.7
These are places designated to have full sunshine during
the period of their most intensive use, and concern areas
that have a high frequency of use and stay. For the whole
inner city, a maximum of two hours on top of the shade
time already found in the present situation applies. There
are also rules for preserving the specific qualities of certain places and a maximum of one hour of shade in them.

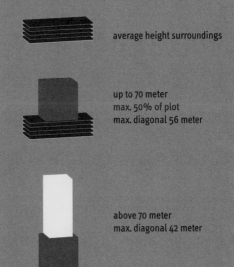

average height surroundings

up to 70 meter
max. 50% of plot
max. diagonal 56 meter

above 70 meter
max. diagonal 42 meter

fig. 6

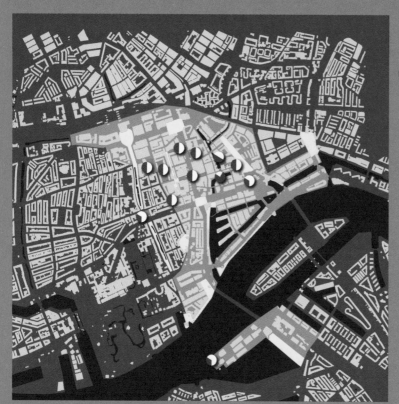

 No deterioration in insolation allowed
12

 Timeframe in which no deterioration is allowed (based on use)
17

Places with specific qualities, minor deterioration allowed

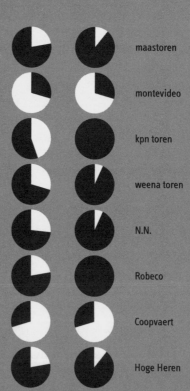

maastoren

montevideo

kpn toren

weena toren

N.N.

Robeco

Coopvaert

Hoge Heren

fig. 7

100   High-rise and Rotterdam

For the wind nuisance an ISO standard has been compiled with verifiable criteria. The question of when to test the maximum allowable winds remains. Usually the extent of the problem is only realized afterwards and a canopy is put in place to offset the situation. To avoid this predicament, wind research must be carried out twice during the planning process. The first time during the master plan phase where high-rise is part of the plan. At this stage volumes can still be moved if they do not meet the standards. Secondly, a wind study has to be done to measure the effects at the building's shape, texture and facade at the preliminary design stage, to test if it is within acceptable limits established in the master plan. →fig.8

Rotterdam's first high-rise vision was a clear statement about the city's image and skyline, and validated the use of high-rise, but the new high-rise vision takes it further. The goal is an inner city that marries high-profile and innovative high-rise with an attractive street life, where high-rise communicates positively with citizens and the street. The new ethos of Rotterdam's high-rise vision can best be summarized by the subtitle of the renewed vision itself: "A city without fear of heights with its feet planted firmly on the ground."

IMAGE SOURCES

All images: Nota Hoogbouw Visie, Gemeente Rotterdam (2010)

fig. 7 Sunspots
fig. 8 High-rise and wind

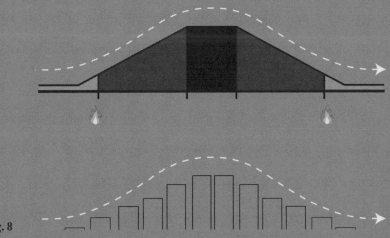

fig. 8

7

Planning and Visibility Assessment of High Building Development in The Hague

Frank van der Hoeven

Steffen Nijhuis

ABSTRACT A true skyline in the Dutch city of The Hague emerged in the spring of 2011 when the construction of four high buildings drew simultaneously to a close: the Ministry of the Interior and Kingdom Relations (146 metres, 2012), the Ministry of Justice (146 metres, 2012), a residential project De Kroon (132 metres, 2011) and a new office tower New Babylon 1 (142 metres, 2011). Together with the Hoftoren (2003, 142 metres) and the Strijkijzer (132 metres, 2007) they constitute a new visual cluster that can be seen by the naked eye as far away as the edge of neighbouring Rotterdam, 16 kilometres away. The Hague's skyline has been four decades in the making. The earliest discussions on buildings to a height of 140 metres date back to the 1960s. Public opinion, fearing the visual impact of such buildings on the city, impeded the planning of such high buildings, while a weak municipal policy was not able to break the stalemate. New instruments that analyse the development of the skyline through time by means of mapping, scatter plots and viewsheds carry the potential to make such public and political debates on high building development more objective, and perhaps less emotional. This chapter presents three such approaches that were developed by the authors: the use of a scatter plot to unravel the dynamics of high building development and height categories through time, the viewshed of the buildings that make up jointly a cluster by means of GISc, and the mapping the outline of the cluster as it appears in the (urban) landscape.

Introduction

The high-rise has been controversial in the Netherlands for years, if not decades. A substantial number of Dutch towns and cities have felt the need to regulate the planning and construction of this specific building type. Because all building activities are regulated in the Netherlands, policy makers and civil servants need a solid framework to guide decision-making in approving or rejecting a high-rise proposal. Various online databases containing data on high-rise buildings show that at least three Dutch cities have a sufficient number of tall buildings or high-rise proposals to justify regulation: Rotterdam, Amsterdam and The Hague. The policy document that emerged in the Netherlands is called *hoogbouwbeleid* or *hoogbouwvisie*. This article analyses the high building policy of the city of The Hague as it was put in place in 2001, ten years ago, and uncovers some inconsistencies in the premise of the policy and assesses the relative visibility of high-rise clusters.

The Hague and its high buildings

The Hague is not the official capital of the Netherlands. It is nevertheless home to the government, the parliament and all of the ministries. The construction of governmental offices is an important driving force behind The Hague's urban development. The volume of office space in The Hague is about 5.5 million square metres. Most of the high-rises here can be found in the city centre. The office rent levels of the two main locations in The Hague's centre (Central Station and Beatrixkwartier) varied in 2009 from €165 to €215 per square metre and from €170 to €200 per square metre, respectively. This is significantly lower than the rent levels in the most prominent locations in Amsterdam, which varied from €250 to €375 per square metre in 2009 area (DTZ Zadelhoff, 2009).

The Hague's 2001 high building policy provided primarily a framework for inner-city development, not for the high buildings in the post-war estates. This may very well explain why The Hague considers a building "high" when its height is equal to or exceeds 50 metres. The tallest buildings in The Hague's post-war estates are 52 metres high.

The Hague started to develop its skyline rather late, only beginning in the early 1990s. At present, it encompasses a remarkable portfolio of high buildings designed by internationally renowned architects.

The initial high building development was hampered by the outcome of an inner-city development that went sour in the 1960s. In the post-war era, two neighbourhoods (Wijnhavenkwartier and Spuikwartier), situated just south of the historical district, were appointed by the city to become the national governmental centre. The proposed development was part of the 1949 strategic urban plan for Greater 's-Gravenhage or the "Plan Dudok" (Schmitt, 2009). It envisioned an underground Central Station to facilitate the scheme. The national government and the Dutch Railways opposed the vision. Slowly, the Wijnhavenkwartier and Spuikwartier started to deteriorate. In the early 1960s, a local tycoon (Zwolsman) proposed a large real estate development based on a master plan designed by Nervi. It included a prominent office tower with a height of 140 metres just at the border of the historical district. The plan was legally contested and rejected (Van der Sluijs, 1989). The proposed tower was subsequently divided in two to accommodate two office slabs of half the size, which currently house the Ministry of the Interior and the Ministry of Justice. A maximum height of 70 metres in the Wijnhavenkwartier and Spuikwartier was introduced to protect a culturally important view of the historic buildings of the Binnenhof, which housed the parliament (Freijser, 2000). In this way, the 70-metre threshold became an important reference point for future developments.

The city has been cautious with regards to high-rise development ever since. In stark contrast to its neighbouring city Rotterdam, there are no proud publications written about the development of The Hague's skyline. City officials tend to be careful when they have to decide on high buildings. For this reason, the high-rise development focused initially on the Beatrixkwartier. This is a peripheral district, safely separated from the inner-city by a double spatial barrier: the Central Station's rail yard and the sunken A12 highway. The construction of the Malietoren (1996, 75 metres) over the sunken A12 was a major milestone for the Beatrixkwartier's development, and was featured in several commercials as an icon for the future Netherlands at the time.

In a later stage, the development shifted back to the Central Station area and the inner city. In 2001, the city presented its proposals for the new accommodation for the Ministry of the Interior and Kingdom Relations and the Ministry of Justice in the Wijnhavenkwartier. Almost ironically, the height of the two towers will be just over 140 metres each. The alderman for spatial planning and urban renewal, Arend Hilhorst, had to defend the proposal in 2002 after a photo-montaged impression, released by the municipality, bluntly falsified the visual impact of the planned high-rises near the Central Station and the Wijnhavenkwartier (Veldhuizen, 2002). The panorama showed a view in which the planned Hoftoren (2003, 142 metres) was clearly reduced in actual size. The towers that would house the new Ministry of the Interior and Kingdom Relations and the Ministry of Justice were barely visible, concealed by elements that seemed to be original elements of the historic parliament building. In fact, the artist's rendering included building elements from a different angle of the parliament; these were pasted into this montage in order to hide the new developments from view. →fig. 1

fig. 1

The affair caused quite a stir in local politics. The alderman survived the controversy and the Hoftoren, which is currently home to the Ministry of Education, Culture and Science, was recognised with multiple awards after it was built, including the 2004 International High-Rise Award (Flagge, 2004). The fact that the local government had to operate from such a defensive stance regarding the visual impact that high-rises would have on the historical district is part of a larger picture here. Because of its prominent historical district The Hague seems to struggle with the difficult relationship between high-rise and built heritage like many towns in the United Kingdom seem to do (Short, 2007), including London (Tavernor, 2007).

Analysis of The Hague's high building policy

The Hague's 2001 high building policy (Dienst Stedelijke Ontwikkeling, 2001) centres on three main components: the architectural heights of building in the city, the high building developments in the various city districts, and possible future developments. In this respect, the document discusses a distinct "Hague Height" *(Haagse Hoogte)*: a typical architectural height between 50 and 70 metres that is said to characterise the city's skyline.

The policy provides a number of reasons why buildings did not exceed this height. One reason is that older policies prohibited buildings higher than 70 metres in the historic city centre. The preservation of a culturally important view of the old parliament buildings prohibited higher buildings. Another reason was the need to maintain an open corridor along the Utrechtse Baan for transmissions from the telecommunication tower that was built in the middle of the Beatrixkwartier. Both restrictions have since been lifted. This is reflected in the new official high buildings policy, which permits buildings over 100 metres in this area. The 2001 policy nevertheless still prohibits the construction of buildings between 70 and 100 metres in height to preserve the integrity of the established skyline. The city seems to cherish its "Hague Height". The high building policy document includes a full-page sketch of the city centre skyline to emphasise this point. →fig. 2

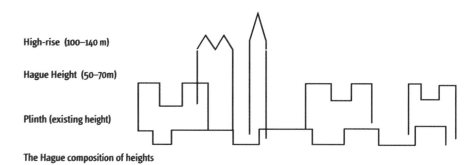

High-rise (100–140 m)

Hague Height (50–70m)

Plinth (existing height)

The Hague composition of heights

fig. 2

Looking at the actual heights of high buildings in The Hague however, there seems to be no such thing as a typical "Hague Height", at least not between 50 and 70 metres. There are several online databases that are available, which contain data on high buildings, most notably the listings at Emporis.com. According to the various websites listed here, in 2001, the year in which The Hague published its high-rise policy, the city already contained eight prominent buildings between 70 and 100 metres high; one building was under construction and three more buildings in this range were proposed. In the same year, The Hague had only one high building over 100 metres. Three similar buildings over 100 metres were under construction and four others were proposed. How is it possible that this policy document is so factually inaccurate in neglecting the existence of tall buildings over 50 to 70 metres? The city's planning officers, external experts and the city council must have reviewed an official document like this. How could they have approved it when it contains such obvious inconsistencies?

The problem may have arisen due to the differing definitions of height. The high building policy document fails to define height *(bouwhoogte)*, which may be measured in many different ways: architectural height, floor-to-ceiling height, floor-to-floor height, highest occupied floor height, main roof height, observation deck height, observation floor height, roof height and tip height (Emporis, 2009).

For instance, the architectural height is defined as "the vertical elevation from the sidewalk level outside of its lowest exposed floorplate, to its highest architectural or integral structural element. These include fixed sculptures, decorative and architectural spires, ornamental fences, parapets, balustrades, decorative beacons, masonry chimneys, and all other architecturally integral elements along with their pedestals" (Emporis, 2009).

Furthermore, the document fails to define a high-rise or a high building. The document also falls short of providing an up-to-date overview of existing and planned high buildings in The Hague. If such an overview was presented in a clear and concise way, then readers could draw their own conclusions whether a typical "Hague Height" truly existed or not.

Because the architectural height is internationally considered to be the official height for primary ranking purposes (Emporis, 2009) this paper takes only the architectural height into account. Data on high buildings can be presented as a simple list or as a scatter plot. This article provides a scatter plot because it can show the relationship between several sets of data. A scatter

fig. 3 **Scatter plot of the architectural height and the year of completion of The Hague's high buildings, including the "official" height categories**

fig. 4 **Scatter plot of the architectural height and the year of completion of The Hague's high buildings, including optimised height categories**

plot is a simple but efficient way to display the relation between two types of quantitative data tagged to a number of specific objects.

Using data on the architectural height and the year of completion of the high buildings, a graph of height (y axis) versus time (x axis) can be plotted. By including buildings under construction and proposed buildings a timeline for high-rise development in a given city emerges. The Hague's scatter plot reveals that the development of high buildings in The Hague began in the late 1960s and remained relatively constant for two to three decades thereafter. Then, in the mid-1990s, architectural heights rose sharply, almost doubling in less than a decade. The diagram clearly shows that there is a context and a rationale for a strategic planning guidance on high buildings in The Hague at the given time.

 residential high-rise

■ black: non-residential high-rise

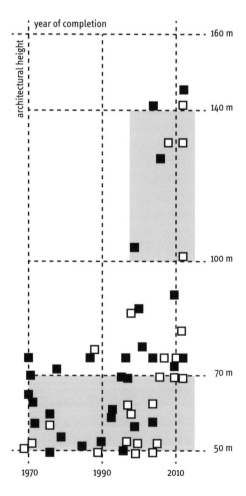

fig. 3

To visualise the relationship between the actual development and the planning guidance, colours can be
added to the scatter plot. Simple rectangles are drawn
to represent the different height categories identified
by the municipality. A rectangle is drawn to indicate the
so-called Hague Height of 50–70 metres, starting in the
data from 1969 and continuing until the present day. The
next rectangle represents the new height range of 100-
140 metres, starting in the data from 1998, the year the
first high building over 100 metres was completed (Cast-
alia, 104 metres). At first glance, this graph looks prom-
ising, but upon further consideration, many of the dots
(each depicting a high building) are still excluded from
one of the two rectangles. It is thus apparent that the
height ranges used in The Hague's high buildings policy
only partly explain what is going on in the city. →fig. 3

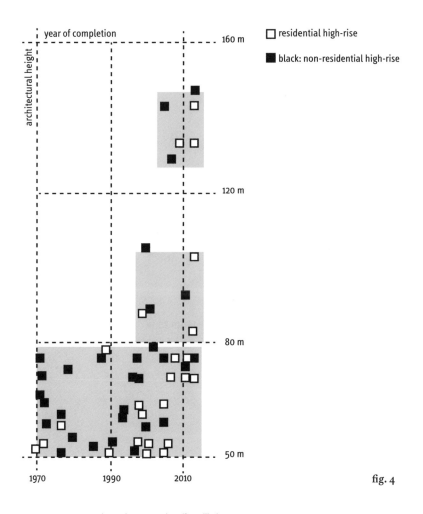

□ residential high-rise

■ black: non-residential high-rise

fig. 4

fig. 5 Map of the inner city of The Hague, the location of existing and future high buildings exceeding 50 metres and the "official" high-rise zoning. The buildings shown belong to categories excluded in The Hague's guidance (70–100 metres, ≥ 140 metres) or belong to the official categories (50–70 metres, 100–140 metres) but are located outside the corresponding high-rise zones

In order to paint a more accurate picture, the Hague Height should be raised to 80 metres, which encompasses most of the buildings built before the mid-1990s. Next, the upper limit of the new category should be raised from 140 to at least 150 metres. The first building in that category, the Hoftoren (2003, 142 metres) and the new buildings that will house the Ministry of the Interior and Kingdom Relations and the Ministry of Justice (146 metres, 2012) are already too high for this category. Similarly, the lower boundary of the category should be raised to 120 metres. A clear frontrunner group of six high buildings now emerges, with a dividing line between 110 and 120 metres that separates them from the rest. This leaves some dots not categorised. These can be accounted for by introducing a third height category, ranging from 80 to 120 metres, which emerged only in the late 1990s. →fig. 4

Instead of two height categories (50–70 metres and 100–140 metres), the city may have to deal with three categories (50–80 metres, 80–120 metres and 120–150

fig. 5

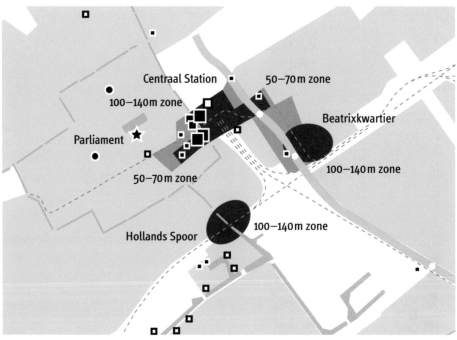

■ ▪ ▪   tall building resp.: over 120m, 80–120m, under 80m
☐ ▫ ▫   (partially) residential tall building: same height range
● ● ·   other tall buildings (bridge, church): same height range

metres). The scatter plot analysis makes this idea appear plausible. So far, the analysis only considered the architectural height and year of completion. The location of a high building within a city is another important dimension of high building policies. For this reason, a second analysis is introduced that looks at the relation between the height categories and zoning in the city. This second analysis takes a fresh look at the area that comprises the cluster of high building in The Hague. →fig. 5

GISc-based visibility analysis

The high level of visibility of high buildings is one of the major reasons to draw up specific policy documents to regulate the development of these special buildings. The joint visual impact of The Hague's high buildings is visualised here in order to determine the area that most influences that visibility.

The visual impact of a high building cluster can be reviewed using a comprehensive GISc-based viewshed method (Rød and Van der Meer, 2009; Nijhuis, 2009; Germino et al., 2001; Nicolai, 1971). The accuracy of this analysis depends on the digital landscape model (DLM), the rule for judging visibility (Fisher, 1991 and 1993; Riggs and Dean, 2007). According to Riggs and Dean (2007), the average level of agreement which can be achieved is up to 85%. These findings suggest that it is better to express the analysis results in terms of probability (Fisher, 1995 and 1996).

However, to achieve the highest degree of reliability, an accurate barrier model or digital landscape model was constructed consisting of a digital elevation model (DEM) in combination with topographic data. The basis is a high-resolution elevation model, the Actueel Hoogtebestand Nederland (AHN-1, 1997–2003), which is precise to about 15 centimetres per square meter. The DEM's density, distribution and planimetric accuracy is such that topographic objects with a size of two by two metres can be identified clearly and with a maximum deviation of 50 centimetres (AHN, 2010). The model has been supplemented with recent topographic data: the digital topographic map at a scale of 1:10,000 (TOP10NL, 2009). All legend items were selected that are higher than eye-level (including ascending elements, buildings

fig. 6 Visual range of high buildings as a function of the relationship between vertical area, shape and contrast value under different meteorological conditions by full daylight. (image source Nijhuis, 2013)

and trees and/or shrubbery) based on the definitions of the Topographic Department of the Land Registry (Topografische Dienst Kadaster). The location, architectural height and year of completion of the high-rise buildings were derived from the Emporis database (Emporis, 2010) and added to the digital topographic map. The resulting digital landscape model was corrected using recent aerial photographs, field visits and Street View imagery (Google Earth, 2010).

A number of parameters influence the result of the GISc-based viewshed analysis. Especially when it comes to high buildings the vertical size (area of the façade) and weather conditions play a crucial role in prediction of probable visibility (Nicolai, 1971). To put it more precisely, the visual range of objects in the landscape depends on: the apparent contrast between the object and its background, the angular size of the object, its shape and vertical area, the contrast threshold at the level of luminance (type of day), the conditions and technique of observing and the eye level and related curvature of the earth (Duntley, 1948; Middleton, 1952). An important factor for determining the maximum visual range of distant objects is the meteorological optical range at different weather conditions. Observations from the Royal Netherlands Meteorological Institute (KNMI) show that the meteorological optical range by full daylight varies from

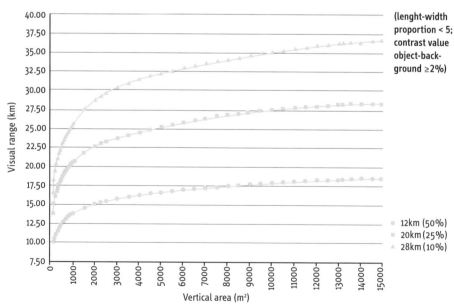

fig. 6

nearly zero up to several tens of kilometres (KNMI, 2010). However, the average ranges of 12 kilometres (50% of the time), 20 kilometres (25%) and 28 kilometres (10%) are typical for Dutch circumstances (Nijhuis, 2013; Nicolai, 1971). For the analysis we calculated the maximum visual range of the high-rise buildings under different meteorological conditions by full daylight and involved vertical area (length-width proportion < 5), vertical shape (rectangular) and contrast value (object-background ≥ 2%). See fig. 6 (Nijhuis, 2013, Van der Hoeven and Nijhuis, 2011). The vertical area was calculated by using fifty percent of the perimeter of the footprint multiplied by the architectural height. The cumulative viewsheds that were from the analysis show the probable visibility at a meteorological optical range of 20 kilometres and takes into account the curvature of the earth. The analysis results were tested for reliability through field visits and photos. →fig. 6,7

The visibility analysis of The Hague's high buildings shows that the collective visual impact of the high building cluster can only be seen at a few isolated spots in the city. Outside the city the combined visual coverage of The Hague's high buildings reaches as far as 5 to 20 kilometres away. The North Sea especially seems the perfect place to observe the skyline. However, the human eye cannot assess the relative position between the individual buildings at a distance of 5 to 20 kilometres. Whether the high buildings are neatly lined-up or randomly positioned is impossible to tell, unless they are all the same size and shape (which they are obviously not). As a result a skyline appears mostly as a two-dimensional phenomenon.

To develop a better understanding of the visual appearance of the city's skyline it is helpful if the geographical coverage of the corresponding cluster is known. To determine this a simple outline can be drawn that links the outer buildings that are supposedly part of the cluster. If a new building is erected within the outline it will not change the width of the city's skyline, regardless the angle from which it is viewed. Any building erected outside the outline does extend the skyline, as seen from a specific angle. Three distinctive height categories were identified in The Hague: under 80 metres, between 80 and 120 metres, and above 120 metres. This means that three of such outlines can be drawn. →fig. 8

fig. 7 Map of the joint visual coverage of
The Hague's high buildings

Visibility buildings > 50 meters

Full daylight: meteorological optical range
20 km (25% of the time)
in relation to vertical size and area
of the building

☐ 1
▨ 1 - 5
▨ 5 - 10
▨ 10 - 50
■ 50 buildings

km
0 1 2 3 4 5

fig. 8 Outlines of the high buildings in the centre of The Hague

The outline that includes the buildings over 120 metres is substantial. The outline for the buildings between 80 and 120 metres is remarkably small. These buildings are all clustered in close proximity to the The Hague's central transit hub. The outline of the buildings between 50 and 80 metres is somewhat larger than the over 120-metre outlines and defines a clear block surrounding The Hague Central Station area.

In the case of most buildings it is clear whether they belong to such a cluster or not due to their proximity to the others buildings. The question is whether the high buildings in the Laakhaven area belong to the area that makes up the visual skyline or not. From some angles these buildings are visually part of the cluster and from other angles they are not. A simple technique can be applied to visualise this. The areas from which a building appears to be part of the cluster (or not) is determined by drawing two lines that connect the building in question with the two buildings that mark the borders of the cluster. If the angle between the two lines is larger than 90 degrees, then the area in which the building appears

fig. 8

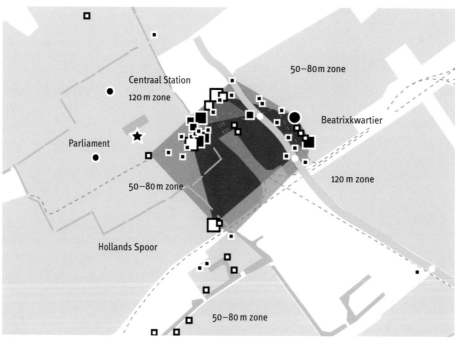

tall building resp.: over 120m, 80–120m, under 80m
(partially) residential tall building: same height range
other tall buildings (bridge, church): same height range

as part of the cluster dominates over the area in which it is visually separated from the cluster. None of the buildings in the Laakhaven area seem to be part of The Hague high building cluster, but one: Laakpoort (50 metres, 1975).

What emerges is a solid block of roughly 1.2 by 1.2 kilometres that seems to define the skyline of The Hague with almost no difference between the lower and the higher height categories. That diagram is radically different from the one that was presented in the 2001 high building policy document.

Conclusions

The development of high buildings in The Hague has been analysed by considering the historical development in relation to the patterns that emerge from architectural height, year of completion, and location in the city of the buildings that measure 50 metres high or more. The height categories that derived from this analysis were used to determine the visual impact that high buildings have on the city and its surrounding territory, and to determine the scope of the high building cluster that seems to determine the development of the city's skyline. The findings contradict the concepts of height categories and zoning used in The Hague's first policy framework published in 2001. Systematic research delivers new and robust height categories (less than 80 metres, 80-120 metres and above 120 metres) and a square shaped cluster that spans the core of the city's high building development. Both findings can be used as a scientific foundation for the city's future policy on high building development.

REFERENCES

— Birmingham City Council (2003). High places, a planning framework for tall buildings. Birmingham: Development Planning Division, Strategic Directorate of Development, Birmingham City Council.
— CABE & English Heritage (2007) Guidance on tall buildings. London. Retrieved Sept 1, 2009 from: http://www. english-heritage.org.uk/upload/pdf/CABE_and_English_ Heritage_Guidance_on_tall_buildings.pdf?1252156283
— CBS StatLine (2009). Retrieved Sept 1, 2009 from: http://statline.cbs.nl/
— Dienst Stedelijke Ontwikkeling (2001) Hoogbouwvisie

Den Haag. The Hague: Gemeente Den Haag.

— DTZ Zadelhoff (2009) Nederland compleet, Factsheets
kantoren- en bedrijfsruimtemarkt medio 2009.
Amsterdam. Retrieved Sept 1, 2009 from:
http://www.dtz.nl/fbi/include/evi_imagebank/img.
asp?id=1923&number=1&object_type=0&src=image

— Duntley, S.Q. (1948) The Visibility of Distant Objects.
Journal of the Optical Society of America 38(3); 237-249

— Emporis (2009) Commercial Real Estate Information and
Construction Data. Retrieved Sept 1, 2009 from:
http://www.eporis.com

— Emporis (2010) Commercial Real Estate Information and
Construction Data. Retrieved from: http://www.eporis.com
[accessed 1 December 2010]

— Fisher, P.F. (1991) First experiments in viewshed uncertainty: the accuracy of the viewshed area. Photogrammetric Engineering and Remote Sensing 57; 1321-327

— Fisher, P. F. (1993) Algorithm and implementation
uncertainty in viewshed analysis. International Journal
of Geographical Information Science 7 (4); 331-347

— Fischer, P.F. (1995) An Exploration of probable
viewsheds in landscape planning. Environment and
Planning B: Planning and design 22; 527-546

— Fisher, P.F. (1996) Extending the applicability of viewsheds
in landscape planning. Photogrammetric Engineering and
Remote Sensing 62 (11); 1297-1302

— Flagge, I. (2004) International Highrise Award 2004.
Hamburg: Junius Verlag.

— Freijser, V. (2000) Stad in vorm, de vernieuwing
van Den Haag 1985-2000. Rotterdam: 010 Publishers.

— Germino, M.J., Reiners, W.A., Blasko, B.J., McLeod, D.,
and Bastian, C.T. (2001) Estimating visual properties of
Rocky Mountain landscape using GIS. Landscape and
Urban Planning 53; 71-84

— Landeshauptstadt Düsseldorf, Stadtplanungsamt (2004)
Hochhausentwicklung in Düsseldorf Rahmenplan,
Beitrage zur Stadtplanung and Stadtentwicklung in
Düsseldorf. Düsseldorf: Landeshauptstadt Düsseldorf,
Der Oberbürgermeister, Stadtplanungsamt.

— Mayor of London (2001) Interim strategic planning
guidance on tall buildings, strategic views and the skyline
in London. London: Greater London Authority.

— Rutten, J. (2007) Stationslocaties, Kathedralen van de
nieuwe tijd. The Hague: Ministerie van VROM

— Middleton, W.E. (1958) Vision through the atmosphere.

Toronto; University of Toronto Press.

— Nicolai, J. (1971) De visuele invloed van woonplaatsen op open ruimten. Met enkele toepassingen op het midden van west-Nederland. Delft, Technische Universiteit Delft.

— Nijhuis, S. (2009) Het visuele landschap, in: Werkboek bouwstenen structuurvisie Noord-Holland 2040. Analyses en Verkenningen 3/3. Haarlem, Province of Noord-Holland.

— Nijhuis, S. (2013) Landscape Architecture and GIS. Geographic Information Science in landscape architectonic research and design. Delft University of Technology (in preparation).

— Riggs, P. D., and Dean, D. J. (2007) An Investigation into the Causes of Errors and Inconsistencies in Predicted Viewsheds. Transactions in GIS 11; 175–196

— Rød, J. K., and Van der Meer, D. (2009) Visibility and dominance analysis: assessing a high-rise building project in Trondheim. Environment and Planning B: Planning and Design 36(4); 698–710

— Schmitt, M. (2009) Maarten Schmitt, city-architect The Hague (NL). Retrieved Sept 1, 2009 from: http://www.schmittsfavorites.nl/2009/interviews.asp?boek_id=3&id=15

— Short, M. (2007) Assessing the impact of proposals for tall buildings on the built heritage: England's regional cities in the 21st century, Progress in Planning, 68, pp. 97–119.

— Sluijs, van der F. (1989) Haagse stedebouw, mijn ervaringen in de jaren 1946–1983. Utrecht: Matrijs.

— Stadtplanungsamt Frankfurt am Main (2008) Hochhausentwicklungsplan Frankfurt am Main – Fortschreibung 2008. Retrieved Sept 1, 2009 from: http://www.stadtplanungsamt-frankfurt.de/hochhausentwicklung-splan_frankfurt_am_main___fortschreibung_2008_5801.html?psid=8a671b2e368cd6267998d0e9945db761

— Taillandier, I., Namias, O. & Pousse, J.F. (2009) The Invention of the European Tower. Paris: Editions A. & J. Picard/Editions du Pavillon de l'Arsenal.

— Tavernor, R. (2007) Visual and cultural sustainability: The impact of tall buildings on London, Landscape and Urban Planning, 83, pp. 2–12.

— Van der Hoeven, F. & Nijhuis, S. (2011) Hi Rise! I can see you. Planning and visibility assessment of high building development in Rotterdam. In: Nijhuis, S., Van Lammeren, R. & Van der Hoeven, F. (eds.) Exploring the visual landscape. Advances in physiognomic landscape research in the Netherlands. Amsterdam, IOS Press.

— Veldhuizen, A. (4th June 2002) Hilhorst tekent toren, Stalin schrapt Trotski, Haagsche Courant.

fig. 1 Ecological Footprint of all countries
in the world

8
High-rise Buildings: A Contribution to Sustainable Construction in the City?

Andy van den Dobbelsteen

ABSTRACT Do high-rise buildings fit into the sustainable city of the future? Life-cycle assessments of highrises compared with low-rise alternatives indicate that, as buildings, high-rises have a bad environmental performance. However, when taking into consideration that land claims beyond the city are avoided and that highrises contribute to more energy-efficient mobility, highrise buildings can prove to fulfil an important role in sustainable cities. This role can be made even more significant by constructing sustainable high-rise buildings, examples of which are already at our disposal. High-rises have further potential to increase the city's productivity by optimally exploiting their vertical surfaces. This article discusses the urgency of developing sustainable cities, the assessment and environmental performance of high-rise buildings, approaches to sustainable highrises, architectural examples of these, and beckoning challenges for the future.

Introduction

The definition of sustainable development, as introduced by the World Commission on Environment and Development (WCED), is often simplified to "a development that

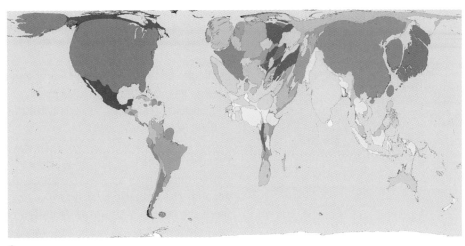

fig. 1

meets the needs of the present without compromising the needs of future generations". In their report Brundtland *et al.* (1987) were a bit more ambitious and clear: sustainable development aims at equity among people across the world and equilibrium between economy and ecology.

A sustainable world
Almost 25 years later we cannot deny that although progress has been made in achieving certain environmental goals, the planet is still severely damaged, there is still no equilibrium, and a more equal spread of prosperity has been limited, reaching only the emerging economies of China, India and Brazil. The western world still uses many more resources than the poorer regions of the world, as the actual ecological footprint of all countries shown in Figure 1 clearly illustrates. →fig. 1

With the limits of what is sustainable being stretched to the maximum, there is simply not enough room to spread the western way of life. In order to accomplish the WCED's objectives (diminished pressure on the environment and increased prosperity across the world), and taking into account the growth of the world population, Speth (1989) and Ehrlich & Ehrlich (1990) calculated that by the year 2040 the environmental impact of our way of life needs to be reduced by a factor of 20. Achieving such a goal in the near future means that planners and designers today will have to work within the confines of

fig. 2 The price of crude oil, early
2006–early 2011 (in dollars/barrel):
we were saved from a severe energy
crisis when the credit crunch struck,
but prices are going up again and expected to rise to 175–200 dollar/barrel

two rather stark limitations, which their predecessors over the past 150 years never had to deal with:

—climate change and related water and heat problems (*e.g.* IPCC, 2007);
—scarcity of resources, especially the depletion of fossil fuels (*e.g.* ITPOES, 2010).

Whether we like it or not, planning and designing for a period longer than 25 years, requires that we take into account the limitations of future resources. Or stated more succinctly: a future-proof design of our living environment will have to be climate-robust and built on renewable or recyclable resources.

Pressing concerns about energy use
Climate change can have devastating effects on the earth (King, 2009), but the depletion of fossil fuels and our heavy dependency on them are the more urgent issues that need to be addressed. As resources are running out, this problem will have radical implications for society. Climate change will contribute to depletion as rising temperatures shift building service demands from heating to cooling facilities – and keep in mind that cooling costs three to ten times more energy than heating.

Local shortages may be solved by importing fossil fuels (particularly coal) from other regions, but this will have some serious ramifications:

—Ethically, do we continue to allow energy sources to be mined, which causes casualties every week?
—Politically, do we want to rely on resources from other, often unstable regions?
—Environmentally, will the extraction of oil and gas from ever deeper wells lead to more accidents?
—Economically, do we want our economy to be reliant on the price of fossil fuel?

With regards to the economic aspect, the price chart of Brent Crude oil →fig. 2 shows us that the credit crunch of mid-2008 practically saved the world from an energy crisis, but also that the price is climbing again at the same rate as in 2008. In that year the chart peaked at $145 a barrel, having never exceeded $100 before. In late April

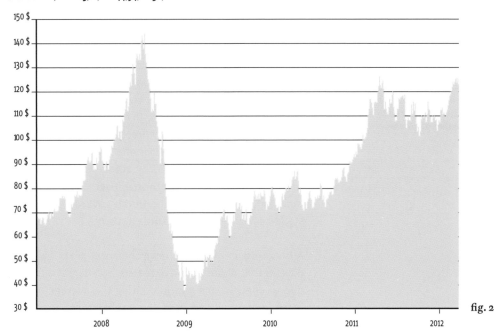

Brent Crude; last 125,61, Hi 144,94, Lo 38,12

fig. 2

2012 it was $125 again. Experts expect future rates to be above $150. Since the price of oil is embedded in everything – energy, materials, products, food, etc. – this will severely affect society.

These effects coincide with the depletion of fuels around the world. Prospects for fossil reserves differ, depending on whether new gas or oil fields can be expected, but Hoogakker (2010) calculated that based on proven reserves the world's energy consumption can be fed for another 55 years, or 75 years maximum if some new known resources are exploited. An average human life is 75 years. Our children and grandchildren will be the victim of our unwise stewardship.

The good news is that we can use up the remaining fossil fuels, but solely for the transition to a sustainable world based on renewable energy. Every new development in the built environment actually needs to be energy-neutral at the very least. Or if we cannot make new buildings energy-neutral, how can we change the existing stock to energy-neutral?

fig. 3 The break-down of the annual environmental load: almost 80% by energy consumption during operation, 20% by the annual write-off and maintenance of building materials, 3% by water consumption

fig. 4 Relationship of stacked building floors and environmental improvement factor, depending on the required net floor area: every size has its environmentally optimal number of stories

Where do we stand: our current environmental performance

If the taxation of our environment needs to be reduced 20-fold and our buildings need to become energy-neutral, then it is worth taking a look at how buildings perform today. In the early 2000s case studies of Dutch government offices revealed that the average amount of progress made since 1990, the first year of reference, was quite limited (Van den Dobbelsteen, 2004). An average improvement to the factor of 1.4 had been achieved while 20 would be required by 2040. A strong S-curve would be necessary to get to that level, especially when taking into account that the Dutch government had installed sustainability measures already.

A break-down of annual environmental costs →fig. 3 indicates that almost 80% of the environmental burden is due to energy consumption during the average 75 year lifespan of a building (Van den Dobbelsteen, 2004). Energy consumption is rooted in three main sources, each contributing approximately 30% to the whole: heating and cooling, lighting, and running equipment. Over the years, the use of equipment – computers, printers, coffee machines, fridges, elevators – has grown from a minor factor in the 1980s, to around 40% of the total today. Demand for heat has diminished, whereas demand for cooling has increased. Lighting remains an important factor. The use of materials for building work also taxes the environment, and around 60% of this is caused by load-bearing structure work. In the case of high-rise buildings, the burden of the supporting structure is of course significant.

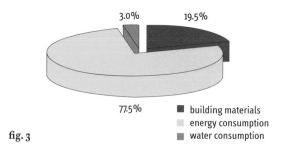

3.0%　19.5%

77.5%

■ building materials
■ energy consumption
■ water consumption

fig. 3

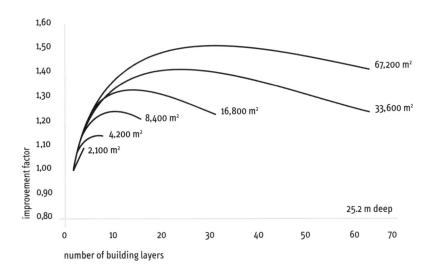

The environmental performance of high-rises

Comparison of building geometries

In order to determine the impact of building geometry on environmental performance, typology studies were conducted (Van den Dobbelsteen *et al.*, 2007) on various building shapes with equal net floor areas (NFA). It turns out that there is an optimal number of floors for every NFA. →fig. 4 The maximum improvement factor is 1.5 (where storeys are max. 25.2 m high) or 1.3 (where storeys are max. 12.6 m high) when the buildings are two storeys. The results for high-rises were less favourable, since the study did not involve analysis of types of supporting structures that differed from existing practice. Hence, the lines exceeding 24-30 storeys are actually less favourable than shown here.

Commerzbank assessment

In order to study the environmental performance of high-rises in more depth, Colaleo (2003) analysed Europe's highest tower at the time: the Commerzbank Headquarters in Frankfurt, Germany. →fig. 5 Compared to similarly sized yet low-rise buildings, the Commerzbank's environmental performance turned out worse. This does not

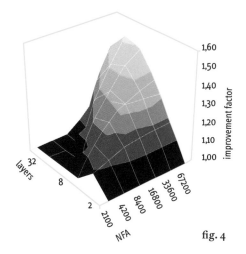

fig. 4

fig. 5 Vertical cross-section and typical floor
plan of the Commerzbank Head-
quarters in Frankfurt, Germany
fig. 6 Three technical dimensions of
sustainability: technology, space
and time
fig. 7 Ways to improve the use of space
in buildings and by the design of
buildings

mean that the Commerzbank tower is bad in its type –
probably not, but we do not know since no comparison
was made with other high-rises.

It is not surprising that energy consumption was high if
you consider all the transportation required for people
and services (air, water, etc.). The main problem however,
lies with the use of building materials in high-rises: foun-
dations need to be deeper and heavier and the structure
is itself heavier. In the particular case of the Commerzbank the columns were also a burden on the performance
assessment. These have the same cross-section dimensions from bottom to top, but the use of reinforcement
steel diminishes on the way up, meaning that more concrete was used than otherwise necessary.

Integrating the three technical dimensions of sustainability

From the above studies, one could conclude that high-
rise as a building type is not sustainable. However, we
would then be ignoring the benefits of less land use and a
longer life of service that such a building can deliver. With
this we come to the core problem of environmental assessments: buildings are commonly assessed by their use
of materials, energy and water, whereas the expected
service life and use of space within the city is ignored. An
assessment less biased towards resources and energies
spent is therefore needed to fully value high-rises.

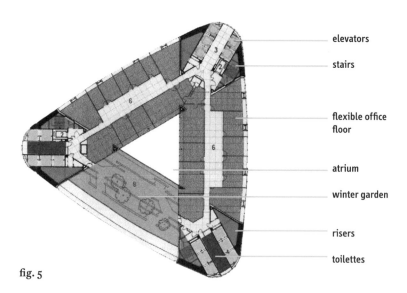

elevators

stairs

flexible office
floor

atrium

winter garden

risers

toilettes

fig. 5

The goal of sustainability can be approached by attempting to improve technological aspects (not just building services, but also the design of buildings), however a consumption reduction by the factor of 20 is much more likely to be achieved through a totally integrated approach to technology, space and time. →fig. 6 Space and time in particular prove to be interesting factors in achieving sustainability, and are indeed advantages specific to high-rise buildings.

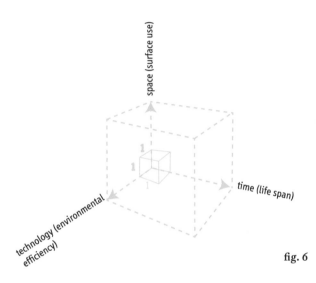

fig. 6

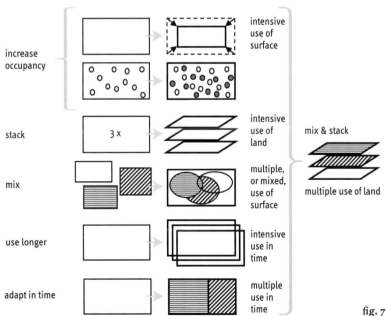

fig. 7

fig. 8 Calculation principle of the Green
       Area Preserved (GAP)
fig. 9 Annual gasoline use as a function of
       urban density, with typical regions
       of the world.

The use of space can be optimised (Van den Dobbelsteen and Wilde, 2004) by increasing the occupancy (intensive use of surface area), stacking (intensive use of land), mixing (multiple or mixed use of surface), using longer (intensive or prolonged use in time) and adapting in time (multiple or sequential use in time). An interesting combination is stacking and mixing (multiple use of land), features of the high-rise. →fig. 7

Green Area Preserved

An important factor when considering the ecological value of high-rises is the Green Area Preserved (GAP). This refers to the open space beyond the city, preserved through building more intensively than on average within the city (Van den Dobbelsteen and Wilde, 2004). Figure 8 graphically illustrates the principle of the GAP. →fig. 8

A high GAP means that spatial claims on surrounding areas have been avoided due to a specific project. If furthermore these areas are ecologically valuable – determinable by the eco-costs of these lands (Vogtländer, 2001) – the performance score will be high.

Density and transport

Another important asset of high densities through high-rises is the proven reduced consumption of fuel for transport in cities that are more densely built than others (Newman & Kenworthy, 1989 & 2001). Figure 9 illustrates this relationship. Eastern Asia, renowned for its

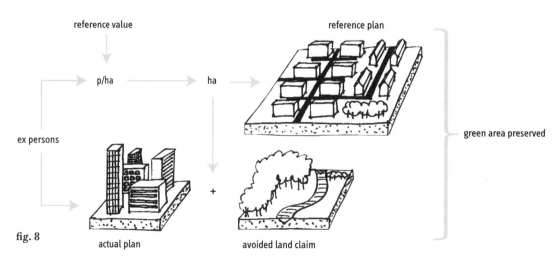

fig. 8

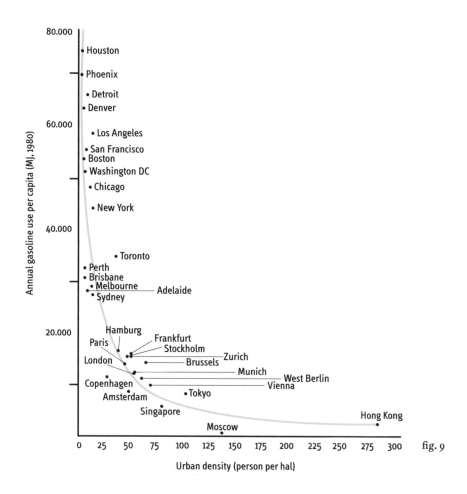

fig. 9

high-rise cities, shows the least consumption of gasoline. So building densely, with the help of high-rises and of course a proper system of public transport or slow routes for bikes and pedestrians, can be an important component in sustainability. →fig. 9

Comparison of redevelopment plans
Case studies in Paris, London and Amsterdam (Van den Dobbelsteen and Wilde, 2004) demonstrated that intensifying and mixing urban areas leads to better environmental performance. Figure 10 gives the environmental improvement factors (with respect to a well-defined average European urban plan) for the use of land, building materials, energy and transport fuel. The effects on land use and transport of these intensified urban redevelopment plans are evident. →fig. 10

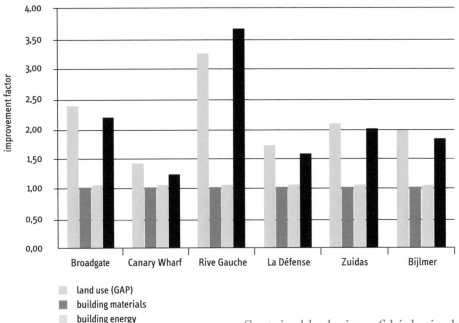

fig. 10

Sustainable design of high-rise buildings

Three directions for energy-conscious design
There are basically three ways we can make buildings more sustainable in terms of energy use:
—Smart & bioclimatic design
—Seizing local potential
    —use renewable energy: sun, wind, hydro, geothermal energy, biomass, etc.
    —use energy more effectively: the low-ex principle, which is to use the right quality of energy for the right demand and re-use waste streams of energy (or other streams) for functions that may still profit from this source.
—Reducing the energy demand: in all case studies conducted by the author, energy-neutrality was attainable through a sustainable production of energy, but half of the assignment always was to reduce the demand in the existing building stock.

Smart & bioclimatic design
Smart & bioclimatic design (S&BCD) is defined as a design approach that deploys local characteristics intelligently for the sustainable design of buildings and urban plans. It is based on earlier definitions of "bioclimatic design" by Ken Yeang (1996) and "smart architecture" (Hinte *et al.*, 2003).

S&BCD is an incremental approach:

1. Definition of bottom-line standards and conditions (for instance comfort requirements and energy performance scores)
2. Study of local circumstances (the local characteristics)
3. Synthesis into a plan with established boundaries (the underlayer before the design starts)
4. Smart design (the fun part for architects and urban planners)

Local characteristics can encompass climatic features (climate type, seasonal changes, variety of the weather, diurnal differences), natural circumstances (geomorphology, hydrology, ecology, natural landscape, soil and ground composition) and man-made interventions (cultural-technical landscape, historical and technical elements, the built surroundings).

All of this seems logical and perhaps even trivial, so why is it important to make it explicit? The answer is simple: everyone knows that climates vary across the world, →fig. 11 and yet why, then, do (especially) office build-

fig. 10 Comparison of six urban redevelopment plans with high densities, assessed by comparison with an average European urban plan. The first two are in London, the second two in Paris and the final two in Amsterdam

fig. 11 Different climates in the world, from left to right: tropical climate, desert climate, temperate sea climate, continental climate and polar climate

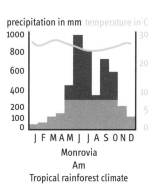

Monrovia
Am
Tropical rainforest climate

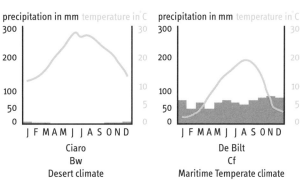

Ciaro
Bw
Desert climate

De Bilt
Cf
Maritime Temperate climate

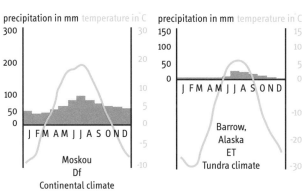

Moskou
Df
Continental climate

Barrow,
Alaska
ET
Tundra climate

fig. 11

fig. 12 Offices look the same everywhere, regardless of their location and orientation
fig. 13 Principle of the New Stepped Strategy
fig. 14 Principle of REAP for urban areas: the New Stepped Strategy that starts with buildings but expand to neighbourhoods and district for optimal balancing of supply and demand before the question of sustainable generation is tackled

ings look the same everywhere? If you look at a random picture of an office building, it is often impossible to determine its whereabouts and its orientation. Offices basically look the same everywhere. →fig. 12

Building structures that ignore local circumstances has been possible only because of the cheap and easy access to energy. Building services behind the façades of office towers have been able to compensate for the design errors made: heating in cold climates, cooling in hot climates or both in versatile climates. As cheap and easy energy continues to deplete, this way of designing will soon be regarded as decadent. For new buildings, locality in design will become a necessity and can present some exciting architectural challenges.

The New Stepped Strategy

The sustainable design of buildings, high-rises included, can be guided through a structured approach with the specifically developed New Stepped Strategy (NSS) (Van den Dobbelsteen, 2008). With respect to the well-known Trias Energetica (Lysen, 1996), the NSS adds an important intermediate step between the reduction in demand and the use of renewable resources, and it incorporates a waste stream strategy inspired by the Cradle to Cradle philosophy (McDonough and Braungart, 2002). The last step of the Trias, which accepts the use of fossil fuels, is eliminated. The New Stepped Strategy is as follows. →fig. 13

fig. 12

The first step is to follow the principles of smart & bio-climatic design as noted above. This means more than just adding thermal insulation. The second NSS step is to optimise waste flows – *using* waste heat, waste water and waste material. The consequence for the third step (the NSS's 3b) is that waste that cannot be processed in our technical waste processing cycle, is therefore to be returned to nature. This can only be done if the waste is safe (non-toxic) and if it can form nutrients for micro-organisms. Lysen's step 3 will continue to be necessary for the coming years of transition, however eventually this will no longer be desirable or even possible. All new buildings should be designed independent of the use of fossil fuels.

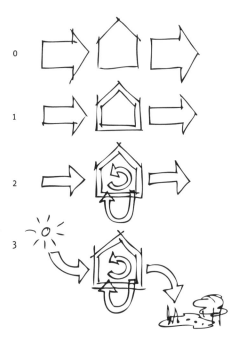

The Rotterdam Energy Approach & Planning (REAP)

Based on the New Stepped Strategy, a team of people from the City of Rotterdam, architects and the Technical University Delft (Tillie *et al.*, 2009a) developed the

fig. 13

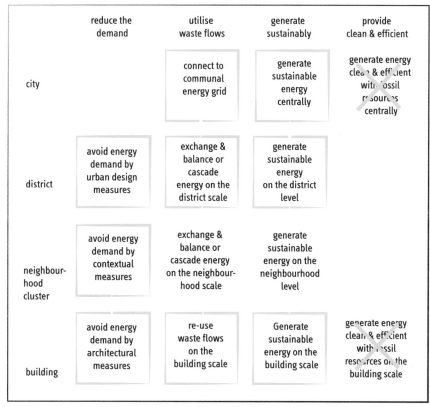

	reduce the demand	utilise waste flows	generate sustainably	provide clean & efficient
city		connect to communal energy grid	generate sustainable energy centrally	~~generate energy clean & efficient with fossil resources centrally~~
district	avoid energy demand by urban design measures	exchange & balance or cascade energy on the district scale	generate sustainable energy on the district level	
neighbour-hood cluster	avoid energy demand by contextual measures	exchange & balance or cascade energy on the neighbour-hood scale	generate sustainable energy on the neighbourhood level	
building	avoid energy demand by architectural measures	re-use waste flows on the building scale	Generate sustainable energy on the building scale	~~generate energy clean & efficient with fossil resources on the building scale~~

fig. 14

fig. 15   Urban functions have totally different energy patterns for heat (h), cold (c) and electricity (e). This image shows that a logical connection between specific functions can be made that require heat or cold, since the generation of cold produces waste heat, which can be used elsewhere but usually is emitted into the air

fig. 16a,b   Synergetic buildings

Rotterdam Energy Approach & Planning (REAP) method for a structural approach to urban areas. The three NSS steps were applied not only to buildings but also to clusters, neighbourhoods, districts and the entire city. Figure 14 graphically illustrates the principles of the REAP method. →fig. 14

REAP was tested on, or actually evolved with, a study of the district of Hart van Zuid (Heart of South), for which the City of Rotterdam wanted to explore its potential to be carbon neutral. The largest harbour city of Western Europe aims to be 50% carbon neutral by 2025, so interventions in the existing urban landscape are necessary. REAP demonstrated that Hart van Zuid could become carbon neutral without demolishing existing buildings, but by a smart exchange of waste energy streams between various urban sites and by adding some greenhouses, green façades and green roofs.

The essential innovation of the REAP method is the step of exchanging, balancing and cascading waste energies in an urban context. In cities, every type of building has its own typical pattern of energy demand and supply. →fig. 15 Optimisation of this equation within a building is useful, but can be much more effective on an urban scale

hospital   h c e

supermarket   h c e

office   h c e

housing   h c e

ice rink   h c e

shop   h c e

school   h c e

swimming pool   h c e

fig. 15

where different waste products (or waste resources) can be matched with each other. Earlier approaches have neglected this as yet untapped energy potential in cities.

Since the 2009 publication of Tillie *et al.* (in Dutch and English), the concept was presented to the Dutch Minister of the Environment, it got national TV and radio coverage, was published in a scientific journal (Tillie *et al.*, 2009b) and inspired other cities to adopt the method.

Smart combinations of buildings

An understanding of energy patterns may lead to novel combinations of energy supply and demand in the existing urban fabric. However, in the case of new buildings and developments the coupling of streams, by-products and uses can be established directly in "synergetic buildings". →fig. 16a,b In these buildings, two functions are energetically complementary: one process eats the waste of the other and vice versa.

Knowing that high-rises are seldom built for a single use, a smart and energy-conscious combination of all the individual functions (offices, apartments, retail, swimming pool, parking garage…) may be a way of creating a sustainable typological architecture. The examples discussed below demonstrate that sustainable high-rise buildings do not have to be designed as separate entities, disconnected from their urban environment. On the contrary, they can play an important role in the city of the future.

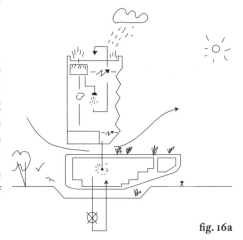

fig. 16a

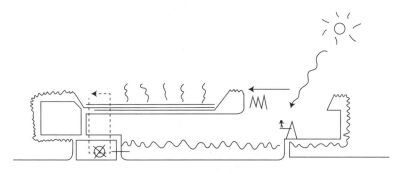

fig. 16b

fig. 17   Ken Yeang's Menara Mesiniaga,
           Kuala Lumpur
fig. 18   National Library, Singapore
fig. 19   EDITT Tower, Singapore
fig. 20a,b Madison Square Park tower

Examples of sustainable high-rises

Ken Yeang, godfather of the bioclimatic skyscraper

With his experience and books on bioclimatic and eco-logical skyscrapers, Ken Yeang is not only the godfather of modern bioclimatic design, but also the ambassador of sustainable high-rises based on bioclimatics. Yeang has designed many inspiring examples of bioclimatic towers, yet regrettably not so many have actually been constructed. Perhaps his best known built example is the Menara Mesiniaga in Kuala Lumpur, built in the 1990s.
→fig. 17

Born in Malaysia, Ken Yeang has learned how to deal with the tropical climate well, and instead of giving in to the supremacy of the air-conditioner, he has sought various ways to cool buildings in a natural way, making optimal use of the local conditions. Tropical climates, as Figure 11 showed, always have high temperatures (typi-cally 25–30°C) and high humidity, exceeding 90% in the rainy season. This means that evaporative cooling is not an option and also that the ground cannot be a tempera-ture resource, as is the case in countries with significant

fig. 17

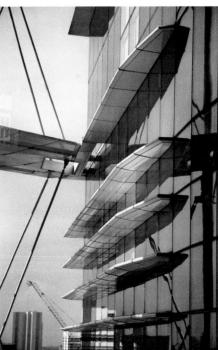

fig. 18

fig. 19

temperature differences between day and night (like deserts) or summer and winter (like temperate and especially continental climates). Cooling in tropical climates must therefore involve measures to avoid rising heat and working with natural cooling via air flows, and to a lesser degree by evaporation and shading provided by plants. This hardly replaces mechanical cooling completely, but a significant contribution can be made.

A good example of Ken Yeang's approach to cooling is the Singapore National Library, →fig. 18 designed as a structure that promotes air current accelerations through the building, thereby bioclimatically cooling the interior by a few degrees which is a great thing when every degree of mechanical cooling costs three to ten times more energy than heating.

Another example is the use of vertical green landscapes whereby plants assist in evaporative cooling, shading and micro-climate improvements, while of course also impacting a stony city in an ecologically positive way (Yeang, 2002). The EDITT Tower, never built, is an example of this. →fig. 19 Plants are a green infrastructure that climb, wind and sway through a building continuously, producing a vertical cocktail of nature and culture.

Yeang copycats
Ken Yeang's green models have since their publication inspired other buildings, but these are mostly weaker versions and seldom relate as intrinsically to the local climate. →fig. 20a,b

fig.20a

fig.20b

fig. 21 Gwangyo Project
fig. 22 Venlo Cradle to Cradle Tower design
and artist impression of the Mumbai
Green Tower: both with more
purposes for the green than just
make-up
fig. 23 Artist impression of Villa Flora,
Venlo

Yeang designed his bioclimatic or ecological towers specifically in response to the natural, local circumstances. The use of greenery by many other architects seems to have very little to do with, or have any real interaction with, the local climate. In these cases the purpose of green was to create an indoor climate and probably to add an aesthetic quality, but fundamentally green behind glass does not interact with the outdoor climate.

Green on the outside of buildings →fig. 21 has also recently become a fashionable solution contributing to carbon neutrality. Plants live off of CO_2 and give back oxygen, thereby compensating for carbon emissions by buildings or the built environment. Certainly an improved micro-climate is a positive contribution.

fig. 21

Vertical agriculture

The use of green in or on buildings, in high-rises in particular, has become a functional, albeit sometimes fashionable, part of recent architectural expression. The potential for purposeful green is still growing, for example with concepts for urban agriculture, indoor water purification and algae production. The Cradle to Cradle principle of aligning man-made practice with natural ones has helped this development. The city has taken from nature and now it should give back, in a more formidable form than ever. →fig. 22

Closing cycles: Villa Flora

The developments described above contribute to the strength of sustainable building and bring us closer towards closing the cycles of materials, water, food and

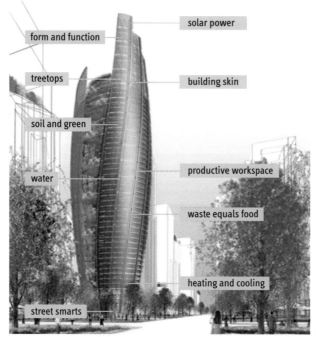

solar power

form and function

treetops

soil and green

building skin

water

productive workspace

waste equals food

heating and cooling

street smarts

fig. 22

fig. 23

energy. The influential Cradle to Cradle book espoused this, but the principles of closed cycles are much older. Early bio-ecological and permaculture movements, to mention but two, have always strived for closing cycles at a specific scale.

Dutch-Icelandic architect-inventor Jón Kristinsson designed a splendid example of a building in which all streams are closed: Villa Flora. →fig. 23 This particular building was constructed for the 2012 Floriade World Horticultural Expo in Venlo, the Netherlands. It is a lowrise, but its concept could easily be applied to a vertical version. The use of parabolic solar collectors would use the limited roof space of a skyscraper and the underground heat and cold storage can easily be employed

fig. 24 Energy system of Villa Flora
fig. 25 Harvest Tower, Vancouver, artist
impression and system of the urban
agriculture

on plots of not more than 150×150 metres. The glazed
greenhouse could be turned up for vertical use. →fig. 24

Urban agriculture in high-rise

Kristinsson's Villa Flora is part of a horticulture exhibi-
tion with no follow up for commercial production, but
serious attempts are currently underway to actually
make buildings for food production, high-rises included.
An example is the plan for Harvest Tower, a sustainable
vertical farm in Vancouver. →fig. 25 Obviously, these limited vertical and horizontal surfaces can never yield as
much produce as commercial farming, but they may pro-

fig. 24

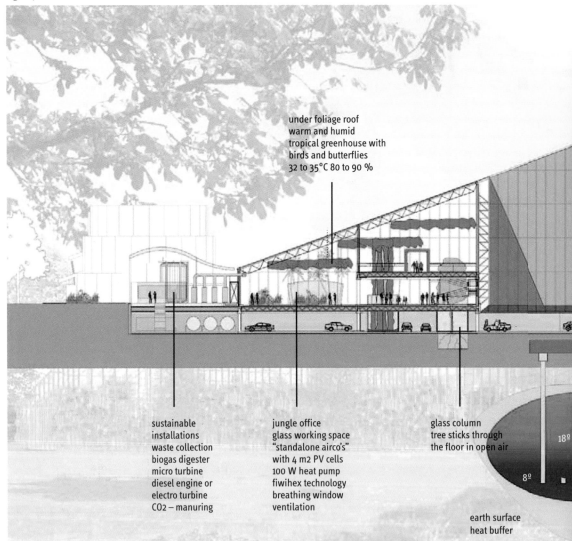

under foliage roof
warm and humid
tropical greenhouse with
birds and butterflies
32 to 35°C 80 to 90 %

sustainable
installations
waste collection
biogas digester
micro turbine
diesel engine or
electro turbine
CO2 – manuring

jungle office
glass working space
"standalone airco's"
with 4 m2 PV cells
100 W heat pump
fiwihex technology
breathing window
ventilation

glass column
tree sticks through
the floor in open air

18º

8º

earth surface
heat buffer

vide a harvest of locally grown fruit, vegetables, herbs and spices.

The trend of returning to locality in smart design is linked to a similar trend in food consumption. Anonymous and untraceable mass production is gradually being replaced by food that we can see and understand again.

An interesting, and to some disturbing, expression of this trend is a conceptual design by Winy Maas of MVRDV, wherein he brings mass production into the city rather than creating a new, miniature version of it as in the example of the Harvest Tower. His Pig Balconies stack

fig. 25

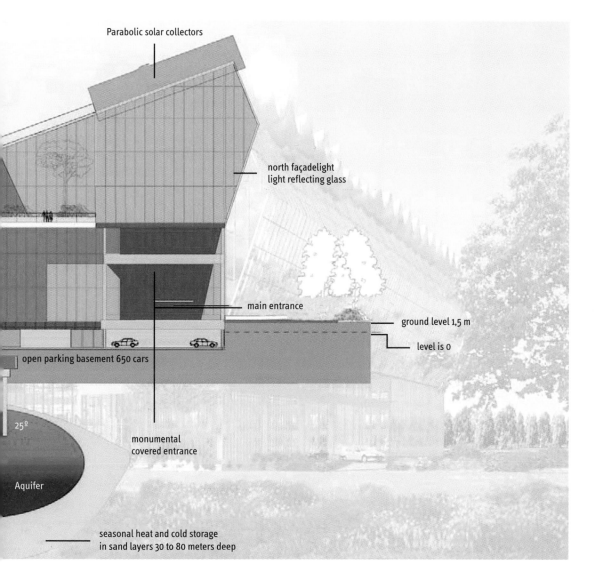

Parabolic solar collectors

north façadelight
light reflecting glass

main entrance

ground level 1,5 m

level is 0

open parking basement 650 cars

25⁰

monumental
covered entrance

Aquifer

seasonal heat and cold storage
in sand layers 30 to 80 meters deep

fig. 26 Miami CON Building

pig farms in skyscrapers, enabling cost-effective meat farming as well as – and this is often misunderstood – a comfortable life for pigs and the means to close cycles within the city. If pigsties were to be incorporated in cities, organic waste flows could be better used: pigs eat food remnants and their manure can be employed for energy purposes (biofermentation to produce biogas). And Maas' message is valid: if eating pork is part of our way of life, why do we not want to see the consequences?

A new challenge for high-rises

It is not all green

The previous examples all seem to relate to a new movement towards nature. However, incorporating green and animals in high-rises is, of course, not a prerequisite for sustainability. It is merely a green translation of the kind of sustainable thinking that could also give shape to much more technical solutions. Figure 26 shows the Miami COR building, by Oppenheim and Büro Happeld, which has wind turbines centred in the façade perforations of its rooftop level, and is a good example of integrating technology with design. →**fig. 26**

fig. 26

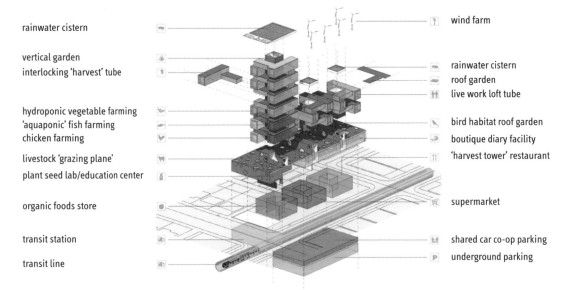

rainwater cistern

vertical garden
interlocking 'harvest' tube

hydroponic vegetable farming
'aquaponic' fish farming
chicken farming

livestock 'grazing plane'
plant seed lab/education center

organic foods store

transit station

transit line

wind farm

rainwater cistern
roof garden
live work loft tube

bird habitat roof garden
boutique diary facility
'harvest tower' restaurant

supermarket

shared car co-op parking
underground parking

The Miami COR building is just an example of how architectural features in a high-rise, in this case the envelope, can contribute to productivity. Here it is not green or food, but energy. This is not a luxury commodity since we understand the urgency of defeating our dependency on fossil fuels. In a sustainable city every square metre of space needs to be purposefully used. High-rises can play an important role in this challenging transition.

High-rises have small roofs but a lot of vertical area
The production of energy, whether it be electricity or heat, has mostly occurred through the use of horizontal space since PV panels, solar collectors and wind turbines are usually arranged in horizontal grids of land or roofs. High-rise buildings have small roofs and therefore provide little opportunity to become productive in this sense.

With this reasoning, the value of vertical surfaces is commonly underestimated. We should understand that countries above the Tropic of Cancer and below the Tropic of Capricorn receive more solar energy on their vertical façades than on their roofs. The farther north, or respectively south, from these lines you place your building, the more productive your façade can be.

To demonstrate this significance in energy terms:
—The Netherlands (52° Northern Latitude) has an average maximal solar angle of 37°, which is more vertical than horizontal. And this only applies to 12 AM solar time; before and after that the average solar angle is of course even lower.
— Free irradiated PV panels and solar collectors directed vertically to the south yield more in wintertime than horizontal ones. Solar collectors placed at so-called optimal angles produce their maximum amount of hot water in summer, when it is least needed. ETH Zürich already found that vertical collectors on east, south and west elevations (in the Northern Hemisphere) produce a constant amount of hot water throughout the year, much more in line with the constant need of hot tap water.
—Not many architects understand that in regards to undesirable solar overheating, the south façade (Northern Hemisphere) is not the real problem as the relatively high solar position is easily blocked by horizontal

canopies, panels or louvres. The real problem (north and south of the Equator) is the eastern and western elevation of a building. The low solar irradiation there presents problems of overheating and luminance. This insolation can therefore best be limited by capturing and storing heat or generating electricity. Yet another reason for vertical productive energy devices, plenty of which can be placed on high-rises.

—In cities sunlight is reflected almost horizontally between buildings, potentially enhancing the yield of vertical PV panels and solar collectors.

And in terms of climate improvement:
—Rain hardly ever falls completely vertically. This means that vertical surfaces can also capture, absorb and make use of rainwater, for plants or passive evaporative cooling, for instance.
—Plants on vertical surfaces can be functional by absorption of fine particles and humidification of the urban air, hence improving the city's micro-climate.

Vertical growth of vegetables and fruit, as in urban agriculture, has already been mentioned. Vertical surfaces are, of course, best suited for commercial and promotional purposes. This underlines the importance of high-rises, for they have plenty of vertical skin. Since from now on every square metre counts, sustainable high-rises will have to prove their validity through the optimal use of surface.

Conclusion: the role of high-rises in a sustainable urbanised world

The studies discussed in this article indicate that as solitary objects, high-rise buildings are environmentally less favourable than their low-rise counterparts containing equal internal space. Further research however also made clear that high-rises allow us to avoid excessive land claims outside the city and that there is plenty of evidence that a dense urban area (with high-rise buildings) supports a more sustainable use of transport.

How the balance tips will be defined by the ecological value or supra-urban land and the facilities for environmentally sound modes of transport. It can be expected, however, that with half of the world population living and working in cities and the UN prospect of this figure rising to 80%, rural lands, either natural, agricultural or recreational will become increasingly valuable as cities grow beyond their current boundaries. High-rises therefore can make a significant contribution to the preservation of green areas and establishment of sustainable transportation.

This does not relieve designers of high-rises of their obligation to build sustainably, meaning climate-proof, energy-neutral and constructed with building materials that form part of a circular economy in which only renewables and 100% recyclable and clean materials take part. Fortunately, the various cases discussed in this article and elsewhere in this book demonstrate that sustainable high-rises are possible. The examples already given, plus the great opportunities still uncultivated – such as a more effective use of high-rise facades – promise a positive future role for high-rises in a sustainable urbanised world.

REFERENCES

—Brundtland G.H. (ed.) *et al.* (1987) (World Commission on Environment and Development). *Our Common Future.* Oxford: Oxford University Press, UK.

—Colaleo V.; Sustainability in numbers for technological building; Politecnico di Torino, Facoltà di Ingegneria, Turin, Italy, 2003

—Dobbelsteen A. van den; The Sustainable Office – An exploration of the potential for factor 20 environmental improvement of office accommodation; Copie Sjop, Delft, Netherlands, 2004

—Dobbelsteen A. van den; "Towards closed cycles – New strategy steps inspired by the Cradle to Cradle approach", in: Proceedings PLEA 2008 – 25th Conference on Passive and Low Energy Architecture (CD-rom); UCD, Dublin, 2008

—Dobbelsteen A. van den, Thijssen S., Colaleo V. & Metz T.; "Ecology of the Building Geometry – Environmental Performance of Different Building Shapes", in: Proceedings of the CIB World Building Congress 2007 (CD-rom); CIB/ CSIR, Cape Town, South Africa, 2007

—Dobbelsteen A. van den & Wilde S. de; "Space use optimisation and sustainability – Environmental assessment of space use concepts", in: Journal of Environmental Management, Vol. 73, Issue 2, November (81-89); Elsevier Science, Oxford, UK, 2004

—Dorling D., Newman M. & Barford A.; The Atlas of the Real World – Mapping the way we live; Thomas & Hudson, 2009

—Ehrlich P. & Ehrlich A.; The population explosion; Hutchinson, London, UK, 1990

—Hoogakker J.; "Energie, de grote urgentie", lecture at post-academic course "Op naar energieproducerende gebouwen"; TU Delft, 2010

—IPCC (Intergovernmental Panel on Climate Change); Climate Change 2007: Fourth Assessment Report; IPCC, Switzerland, 1 February, 2007

—ITPOES (Industry Taskforce on Peak Oil & Energy Security); "The Oil Crunch – A wake-upcall for the UK economy", on: http://peakoiltaskforce.net, 2010

—King D.; keynote lecture at SASBE2009; TU Delft, 2009

—KNMI; Klimaatatlas 1970-2000; KNMI, De Bilt, 2006

—Lysen E.H.; "The Trias Energetica – Solar Energy Strategies for Developing Countries", in: Proceedings of the Eurosun Conference (); Freiburg, 1996

—McDonough W. & Braungart M.; Cradle to Cradle – Remaking the Way We Make Things; NorthPoint Press, 2002

—Newman P. & Kenworthy J.; "Sustainable Urban Form: The Big Picture", in: Williams K., Burton E. & Jenks M. (eds.), Achieving Sustainable Urban Form (109-120); Spon Press, London, UK/New York, USA, 2001

—Newman P.W.G. & Kenworthy J.R.; Gasoline consumption and cities – A comparison of U.S. cities with a global survey and some implications; Murdoch University, Murdoch, W.A., USA, 1987

—Speth J.G.; "Can the world be saved?", in: Ecological economics vol. 1, 1989 (289-304)

—Tillie N., Dobbelsteen A. van den, Doepel D., Jager W. de, Joubert M. & Mayenburg D.; REAP – Rotterdam Energy Approach & Planning; Rotterdam Climate Initiative, Rotterdam, 2009a

—Tillie N., Dobbelsteen A. van den, Doepel D., Jager W. de, Joubert M. & Mayenburg D.; "Towards CO_2 Neutral Urban Planning – Introducing the Rotterdam Energy Approach and Planning (REAP)", in: Journal of Green Building, Vol. 4, No. 3, summer, 2009 (103–112)

—Vogtländer J.G.; The model of Eco-costs/Value Ratio – A new LCA based decision support tool; Gopher, Groningen, Netherlands, 2001

—Hinte E. van, Neelen M., Vink J. & Vollaard P.; Smart
   Architecture; 010 Publishers, Rotterdam, 2003
—Wilde S. de & Dobbelsteen A. van den; "Space use optimisa-
   tion and sustainability – Environmental comparison of
   international cases", in: Journal of Environmental Manage-
   ment, Vol. 73, Issue 2, November (91-101); Elsevier Science,
   Oxford, UK, 2004
—Yeang K.; The Skyscraper Bioclimatically Considered – A
   Design Primer; Academy Editions, 1996
—Yeang K.; Reinventing the Skyscraper – A Vertical Theory of
   Urban Design; Wiley-Academy, Chichester, UK, 2002

IMAGE SOURCES

—{fig. 1} Worldmapper.org
—{fig. 2} Digital Look
—{fig. 5} Foster & Partners
—{fig. 9} (Based on:) Newman & Kenworthy, (1989)
—{fig. 10} Wilde & Dobbelsteen (2004)
—{fig. 11} Wolters Noordhoff (2007)
—{fig. 12} Hellman (1994)
—{fig. 13} Dobbelsteen (2008)
—{fig. 14} (Based on:) Tillie et al. (2009a)
—{fig. 15} Tillie et al. (2009a)
—{fig. 16} (Drawings by:) Marc Joubert of JA (2008)
—{fig. 17} TR Hamzah & Yeang
—{fig. 18} TR Hamzah & Yeang; pictures by the author
—{fig. 19} TR Hamzah & Yeang
—{fig. 20} Daniel Libeskind
—{fig. 21} MVRDV
—{fig. 22} McDonough & Partners and Nita & Mukesh Ambani
—{fig. 23} Kristinsson Architects & Engineers
—{fig. 24} Kristinsson Architects & Engineers
—{fig. 25} Romses Architects
—{fig. 26} Oppenheim & Büro Happeld

fig. 1 Metropolis

9
Sustainable High-rise in Dutch Cities

Kees Kaan[1]

What is sustainable?

The first question that arises when talking about sustainable high-rise is whether high-rise can be sustainable at all. Buildings can be qualified as such by a certain energy label, but that does not automatically mean that this sustainability is contextually legitimate. If you build a high-rise office you can get a very good label, but you could still be making a bad choice. Look for example at the city of Rotterdam which is currently tackling the question of whether to continue building high-rise offices in the city centre while there are so many empty buildings. Some developers say we should tear down offices that are in the wrong place. So apparently a sustainable building could be built in the wrong location and therefore ultimately become useless. Defining categories of sustainability is a very good way of identifying positive attributes in buildings. It is a tool that keeps the pressure on making good sustainable projects, but the labels do not cover all the factors that determine if a building is sustainable.

[1] This article is based on an interview with Kees Kaan on Tuesday 27 March 2012. In 2010 Kaan gave a lecture on the topic of sustainable high-rise in the Dutch context. The lecture was part of the sLIM course High-Rise in the Sustainable City. "I made the base of this lecture some 10 years ago because everyone was talking about density without being very precise."

The amount of empty offices in the Netherlands has never been so high. During the recent boom there were many financial incentives to keep developing and building. It was cheaper for users, and more attractive as well, to move to a new up-to-date building rather than stay in an old one. The driving force behind all this was the financial bubble that provided too much money: investors were literally hunting for investment projects. Simultaneously the national government had delegated planning responsibilities to the provinces and municipalities. Now the provinces say that they have some influence, but that most influence lies with the municipalities. In their turn, the municipalities say that they only have the land-use plans *(bestemmingsplannen)* and if the land-use plan allows it, there is nothing they can do about it. If you combine all the land-use plans in all the different municipalities in the Netherlands, you discover that we can still build 10,000,000 m² of office space. The national government has very little influence on these land-use plans, or at least they do not have the political will to do something about it.

fig. 1

fig. 2 New York
fig. 3 Rotterdam

Dream of the metropolis

→fig. 1 Since the second half of the 19th century people have had this dream of the metropolis. They have a fascination with this high density urban environment. Apart from the economic forces that drove urban expansion, we also have a deeply rooted admiration for cities. Out of this rational and sentimental force, the phenomenon of mid-town Manhattan emerged as one of the first places in the world where the dream of the high-rise city was partially realised. If you look at New York now, you can see it as a future that did not happen: the future metropolis looks old. It seems that contemporary high-rise developments still cling to this futuristic vision, but that the reality of land use and density does not match it.→fig. 2

fig. 2

fig. 3

Shifting land use

The Fifth Nota (National Spatial Planning Strategy, 2001) contained data on Dutch land use over the last 120 years. It revealed that urban land and infrastructure have grown dramatically. Land for forest, nature and water have all been reduced while agricultural land use has remained more or less constant. Apparently farmers have a very strong lobbying position in national politics. Within the next 30 years a quarter of land in the Netherlands will again change in use. It seems we are constantly reshaping our small country.→fig. 3

So why do we use more and more land for urban development and infrastructure? It is of course because of demographics. The population has grown since the end of the Second World War, but also the number of people per household has decreased. Furthermore, we have become wealthy, leisure time has increased tremendously and our mobility has exploded along with it. Modern society increasingly requires a specific type of space for a specific type of use. Public space for example is relegated into different kinds of traffic. And our building stock has become more and more specific. Moreover, the increas-

fig. 4

ing demand for guarantees on safety and security has led to an exaggerated level of specification. Each activity or program demands its own space. Only recently has there been a revival of the notion of "shared space". A phenomenon that used to be very common is now considered an innovation. If we need specific facilities for activities like living, working, leisure, education, health and other needs, then we need a lot of buildings and a tremendous amount of infrastructure. In short, the space needed per capita has grown probably much faster than the densification process as a result of urbanisation. And the densification process is actually moving away from creating density.

A density of emptiness

This is a peculiar situation. Density statistics on the scale of the whole country show that we live in one of the most densely populated countries in the world, equal to Japan. But our relatively small cities are not among the densest at all. So apparently our country is like one big city with medium density. As a result it is not so clear how we define what is urban and what is not. "Urban" has become a unique network of urbanisations in a permanent state of change. →fig. 4

We are constantly fighting for space in this country, but why? There seems to be plenty of space. The Netherlands did not have the sort of explosive urban developments like London, Paris or Berlin did in the 19th century. Its urban network developed in the 17th century and expanded in the 20th century, during which time society was transforming from an industrial to a service-based economy. At this point ideas about urban planning had changed completely from the 19th century. Modernism had replaced all previous approaches.

In our profession the issue of density became apparent some ten years ago. Everyone was talking and writing about density, but without being very precise. I did not understand why we were considering densification when Dutch cities are still so empty. Whether you are in Rotterdam or Amsterdam it is always quiet on the streets. When you compare these cities to a real metropolis our density is nothing. What we are doing is developing a density of projects that are either superspacious or left empty. We have the luxury of building something for every need and then building all the roads in between. We are building huge new hospitals, but the number of people has not increased.

Striking FSI

The Rotterdam neighbourhood Zuidwijk consists of 8 quadrants, mostly owned by housing corporations. Our architectural practice, Claus and Kaan, were asked by the Vestia corporation to design the transformation of De Burgen quadrant. This large-scale operation was possible because of this concentrated ownership. The municipality and Vestia wanted to demolish 1000 apartments and replace them with low-rise, but with indoor parking. We developed an interesting concept for the project introducing a collective garden as a tool for diminishing the amount of open public space while at the same time preserving the beautiful green infrastructure of the neighbourhood. At some point I sat down to calculate what was actually happening. The objective was to tear down 1000 homes of $60\,m^2$ each and replace them with 800 homes of $120\,m^2$ and an additional 1200 parking spots. When the original plan was built 50 years ago, 3 to 4 people lived in one house. Now we live with 1.3 people

fig. 4 **Fighting for space?**

in one house. Where 4000 people once lived, there was now space for 1000. So comparing the original plan to the new plan the density of concrete increased 2.5 times for 4 times fewer people: the density decreased by a factor of 10 just to accommodate our new wealth and lifestyle. We densify to make it emptier! →fig. 5

Rudy Utyenhaak explains in his book *Steden vol ruimte (Cities Full of Space)* that this factor 10 is actually a factor 12, so my calculation is even conservative. Utyenhaak continues that the benefit of increasing density depends on some rules. Because of these rules, mostly related to daylight, there is an optimum block height, which is around 8 to 9 storeys.

So why build high-rises if, as Utyenhaak claims, it is not leading to higher density? And if high-rise is not very sustainable as a typology, why would you do it? Is high-rise a hype that reflects our dream of the metropolis or is it an economic necessity? Some people say that no high-rise ever built was financially sustainable.

The problem with Utyenhaak's theory is that it is based on a *tabula rasa*. It works for extensions and area developments in which large plots of land are available. In an existing city we rarely get the chance to build ideal blocks on a blank slate. We have to work within the confines of small vacant plots and densify by doing high-rise acupuncture in the city's urban tissue. And surrounding such developments are existing buildings and their inhabitants.

fig. 5 1.3 persons/house

Political climate

During the 20th century with its social-democratic ideology there was a definitive belief in *maakbaarheid*, or the ability to mould a better society. Planning and building was a not just an activity to create cities, but also an tool to shape our society. During several decades planning decisions were made at a governmental level on the basis of a long-term ideological vision, while the cities and large housing corporations were responsible for the implementation. Today we work in a political reality that is dominated by market forces. Urban development is now driven by private initiatives and crazy ideas. This reduces the chances of planners and architects to operate in a sustainable way. We can measure sustainability on the scale of a single building, maybe even on the scale of an area development, but on the wider scale there is a lack of coherence. The political climate is populist and opportunistic. Long-term visions are lacking and thorough master planning is no longer common. This has been replaced by fluffy statements in which ambitions are expressed without doing the proper research and the tools to achieve them are not supplied, leaving responsibility to an unspecified market. Thus fashion and labels rule in planning and architecture.

The issue addressed in this presentation is about densification. The question is if it is an appropriate strategy to meet today's needs in terms of a sustainable urban environment, and whether high-rise can contribute to this. However, we are living now in a society in which the market decides what is good. And market forces can eschew the balances necessary for sustainability.

The statistics of Rotterdam's city centre tell us that the balance between living and working is off. There are around 60,000 people working in the city centre and only around 30,000 people living there. In Amsterdam this ratio is more or less 50:50. To compensate the imbalance Rotterdam should build at least 10,000 more dwellings in it city centre, the equivalent of around 2000 residen-

fig. 6 Amsterdam and Rotterdam skylines
fig. 7 Measuring densities

tial storeys or 100 towers of 20 storeys high. It is interesting to compare Amsterdam and Rotterdam because Amsterdam chose, quite some time ago, to emphasise medium high buildings rather than high-rise in the city centre. For their urban expansion, they built on surrounding islands and took the Amsterdam typology of canals and narrow row house buildings as a reference to achieve higher density. For IJburg a mix of the Amsterdam Zuid typology and an Anglo Saxon city grid was used. Amsterdam is expanding within its own tradition and has a very clear DNA. Rotterdam with its relatively empty and open city centre and a high open-to-closed space ratio chose the high-rise road. Now that we know we can have the same densities in either, we see that it's a choice whether to use high-rise for densification or not and that the choice depends on the existing urban tissue and the city's existing cultural climate regarding high-rise. →fig. 6

The problem with Rotterdam's strategy of high-rise acupuncture is that it cannot draw on traditional knowledge because it is such a new typology for the Netherlands. Its projects tend to be prototypes with all the consequences. The city's most natural choice is to perform acupuncture, more or less since it is the only way to transform the statistics and reclaim the balance in the inner city. It is also very proud of its image as a young high-rise city.

Mismatch of ambitions and rules

Everything is getting bigger: people are bigger, cars are bigger, televisions are bigger, and homes are getting bigger and bigger. It costs more energy to make buildings bigger and to build the infrastructure that connects everything. If the city sprawls, mobility soars and we need even more space for infrastructure. If we build higher, more infrastructure goes into the buildings. The bill for this extra cost however cannot be handed over to the government. Intuitively we may feel that the more compact we build, the better. However, in order to im-

Three building patterns with a density of 75 dwellings per hectare

○ community facilities
○ shops & workspaces
● maisonettes
○ houses
○ apartments

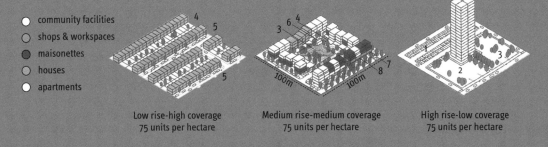

Low rise-high coverage
75 units per hectare

Medium rise-medium coverage
75 units per hectare

High rise-low coverage
75 units per hectare

Different indicators of density: FSI, GSI, OSR and L

The FSI expresses the intensity of an area.

The GSI expresses the compactness of an area.

The OSR expresses the openness and the pressure on the non-built space.

L expresses the average number of floors in an area.

FSI
Floor Space Index

gross floor area/
plan area

GSI
Ground Sapce Index

built area/plan area

OSR
Open Space Ratio

(plan area-built area)/
gross floor area

L
Layers

gross floor area/
built area

fig. 8   Ambition is not a guideline!
fig. 9a,b Chicago

plement high-rise in the existing city in a sustainable way we need more typological knowledge. The ambition must be fuelled by knowledge. Knowledge of urban design and planning on the scale of a normal urban block is readily available, but we are still beginners when it comes to high-rise. Urban planners cannot do this research because it is too architectural, but architects are not doing it either, so the sustainability of high-rise in a Dutch context (i.e. medium density on a medium scale) remains unexplored territory. A lot of research by design is needed to close the knowledge gap. →fig. 7

On top of that there is a mismatch between the spatial ambitions we have and the rules we create to achieve these ambitions. Rotterdam's high-rise vision defines rules without an awareness of the consequences. Its expressed ambitions do not match its rules and policies. Simply stating ambitions without facilitating their implementation is like sitting in the backseat of a taxi giving directions to the driver without a map of the city. Some of Rotterdam's projects have not materialised because

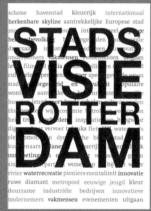

fig. 8

of this. Yet the building industry cannot wait. It's basic economics that they must continue to pour concrete. So at the end of the day projects are built in the places of least resistance and our sustainable city cannot become reality since the market decided. If the city cannot facilitate the ambition it claims to have it will simply not happen. →fig. 8,9a,b

fig. 9a

fig. 10 Fifth Nota versus Rotterdam
High-rise vision

fig. 10

The dilemmas of
the procedural landscape

The planning procedures we have in place do not match the current question of densification and urban transformation. They were made for the development of extensions and large-scale urban area development, but they are not useful for the scale of complex urban projects. The usual legal procedures needed to make a project happen are also an opportunity for local city dwellers to slow it down. Urban residents often enjoy what the city has to offer, but they do not realise that its vitality is sustained by the constant renewal of facilities and new projects. All too often locals do not want high-rises in their backyard and they use all the legal tools available to block development. Since politicians always seem to lean towards the *vox populi*, the broader interests of the general public is underrepresented in these cases. The lack of political backbone causes uncertainties that in turn slow down these projects and are finally never developed because they take too much time. Only when there is a smooth process with clear objectives and a long-term vision backed by local politics do they stand a chance. In summary, there are at least three reasons why large projects in the city tend to stall: lack of knowledge, long regulatory procedures, and political uncertainty. →fig. 10

fig. 11 Rotterdam's skyline evolution
fig. 12 Naïve desire?

Because of the current economic malaise some of these issues have been put aside, but these questions will come back when the economy picks up. The problem with huge projects, like building 100,000 m² or more in the city, is that they take very long to finish and therefore have to be phased. Potential users will not sign an open-ended contract, not knowing when the delivery date of the project is, so developers must provide clarity to potential users and obtain signed lease contracts to get investors interested. In some Rotterdam projects in

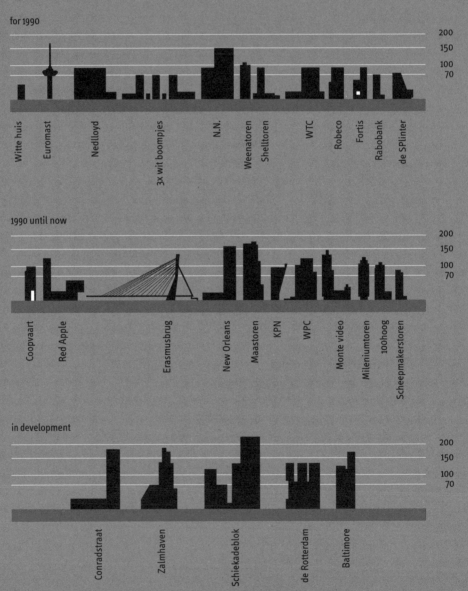

for 1990

200
150
100
70

Witte huis
Euromast
Nedlloyd
3x wit boompjes
N.N.
Weenatoren
Shelltoren
WTC
Robeco
Fortis
Rabobank
de SPlinter

1990 until now

200
150
100
70

Coopvaart
Red Apple
Erasmusbrug
New Orleans
Maastoren
KPN
WPC
Monte video
Mileniumtoren
100hoog
Scheepmakerstoren

in development

200
150
100
70

Conradstraat
Zalmhaven
Schiekadeblok
de Rotterdam
Baltimore

fig. 11

fact, the municipality stepped in to guarantee the project for the investor or signed a lease in order make the project possible. →fig. 11 The inevitable phasing can lead to breaking the project down further into smaller units of development, such as 20,000 m², which is more or less the size of a small single tower. In the case of a single tower, the indoor parking never fits in the building's footprint. As a result the parking will occur at ground level – the most vital and vulnerable part of the city. Several projects in Rotterdam were built this way. This and other issues can only be addressed on a scale larger than a single project. If we can simplify the procedures and shorten the development time for larger projects, there is a chance that people might sign on the dotted line and that we can improve the vitality of our cities. →fig. 12,13

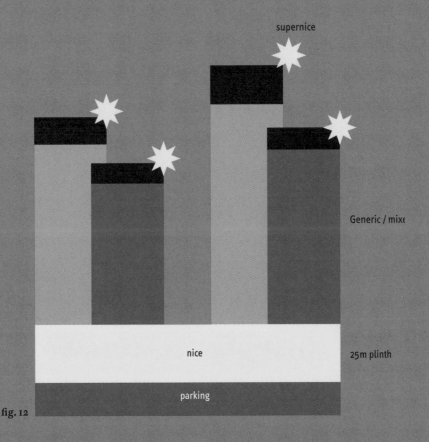

supernice

Generic / mixe

nice

25m plinth

parking

fig. 12

fig. 13 Reality.

Need for a high-rise culture

We can use densification in our cities as a tool to better utilise our existing infrastructure, make cities lively places and perhaps slow down unnecessary sprawl. However, there are many real problems that need to be solved at the conceptual stage of large projects. If we want to build high-rises our priority should be to generate the required knowledge. At the same time, the issue of sustainability within this typology cannot be addressed by looking at one project in isolation. The concept of high-rise as a typology must be analysed within a broader urban environment. As long as we do not develop a real high-rise culture or agree on what densification really means for the Netherlands, we will not be able to address any real densification issues.

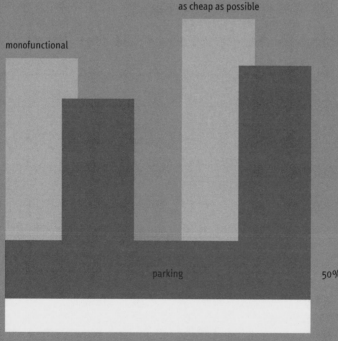

fig. 13

—{fig. 1} Eric Kettelhut, Cityscape for Metropolis – version 1

—{fig. 2} Midtown Manhattan Skyline, New York City – Photo
Postcard A. Mainzer

—{fig. 3} Gemeente Rotterdam (ds+V)

—{fig. 7} Meta Berghauser Pont en Per haupt, Spacemate
– the spatial logic of urban density, 2002 (top illustration)
Andrew Wright Associates, Three ways of achieving
the same density, from A+t, Densidad – density, 2006
(bottom illustration)

—{fig. 8} Gemeente Rotterdam, Stadsvisie Rotterdam
– Ruimtelijke ontwikkelingsstrategie 2030, 2007

—{fig. 9a,b} Michael Wolf, The Transparent City, 2007

—{fig. 10} Gemeente Rotterdam, Herziening Hoogbouwvisie
binnenstad 2010. Ministerie van Volkshuisvesting –
Ruimtelijke Ordening en Milieubeheer, Ruimte Maken,
Ruimte Delen – Vijfde Nota van Ruimtelijke Ordening
2000–2020, 2001

—{fig. 11} Gemeente Rotterdam, Herziening Hoogbouwvisie
binnenstad 2010

—{fig. 12} Claus en Kaan Architecten

—{fig. 13} Claus en Kaan Architecten

10
The Eco Skyscraper: Designing Sustainable Intensive Buildings

Robert Powell

ABSTRACT This essay traces the progressive development of the Eco skyscraper as a sustainable built form with examples drawn from the work of T.R. Hamzah & Yeang (TRHY) in Kuala Lumpur and Llewelyn Davies Yeang (LDY) in London. One of the major challenges in an architectural practice is how to develop a continuous programme of research given the cyclical nature of the economy and the disparate requirements of individual clients. TRHY and LDY resolutely pursue an agenda to create Eco skyscrapers in a continuously evolving research programme. Nature without humans exists in stasis. To achieve a similar state of stasis in our human built environment, must we design our buildings to be like ecosystems? Ecosystems have no waste for everything is recycled within the system. By imitating this function (ecomimesis), our built environment will produce zero waste. Its products will be reused, recycled within the system and when emitted be reintegrated with the natural environment.

In 1976 Yeang set up practice with Tengku Robert Hamzah as T.R. Hamzah & Yeang (TRHY) and by 1986 Yeang had completed three skyscrapers in the Malaysian capital. He also built a residence – the Roof Roof House – on the outskirts of Kuala Lumpur that was a test bed for the principles he would apply to high-rise towers. Orientation, response to sun path and wind directions, sun shading, a double roof, adjustable parts that can be manipulated to achieve cooling by the Venturi effect, evapo-

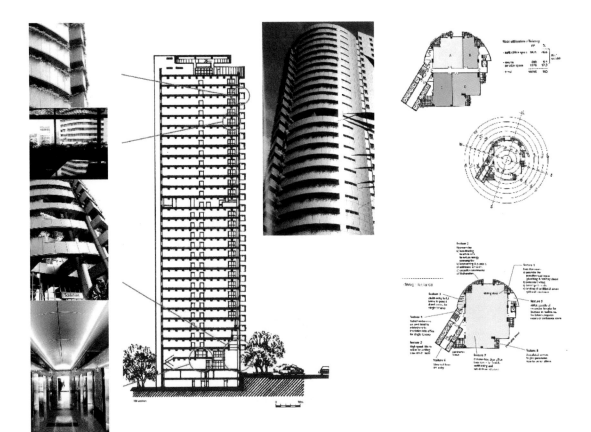

rative cooling, the idea of the wall as an "environmental filter", and natural ventilation were all incorporated. All this early inventiveness finds its way into later ecosky-scrapers.

The skyscraper is not an ecological building type. It re-quires greater material content in its structural system to withstand the bending moments caused by the wind speeds at the upper reaches of its built form, greater energy demands to transport and pump materials and services up the building working against gravity, addi-tional energy consumption for the mechanized move-ment of people up and down its elevators, and other as-pects arising from its verticality. The justification for the ecoskyscraper is that the tall building is a building type that is here to stay and skyscrapers will continue to be built prolifically to meet the demands of city growth and increasing rural-to-urban migration.

THE TROPICAL VERANDAH CITY

SOME URBAN DESIGN IDEAS FOR KUALA LUMPUR

KEN YEANG

Asia Publications

Ecodesign is designing for bio-integration. Within our practice we commence by looking at nature. Nature without humans exists in stasis. To achieve a similar state of stasis in our human built environment we must design our buildings to be like ecosystems. Ecosystems have no waste, for everything is recycled within the system. By imitating this function, our built environment will produce zero waste. Its emissions and products will be

reused, recycled within the system and when emitted be reintegrated with the natural environment. In tandem with this is the need to increase efficient uses of non-renewable energy and material resources.

The process of designing to imitate ecosystems is called ecomimesis. The built environment must imitate ecosystems and that is what Eco skyscrapers must attempt to do.

Yeang's premise is that we must not be seduced by technology. The popular perception is that if we assemble in one single building enough gadgetry such as solar collectors, photo-voltaics, waste recycling systems, building automation systems and double-skin façades, we will instantaneously have ecological architecture. Yeang asserts that although technological systems are relevant in an ecologically responsive built environment, their assembly into one single building does not make it automatically ecological.

Fundamentally, ecodesign is designing the skyscraper as a system integrated within the natural environment. This is the focus for designing sustainable Intensive buildings and it is the basis for TRHY and LDY's approach to ecoskyscrapers as described in Ken Yeang's book *Eco Skyscrapers II* and *Eco Architecture: the work of Ken Yeang*.

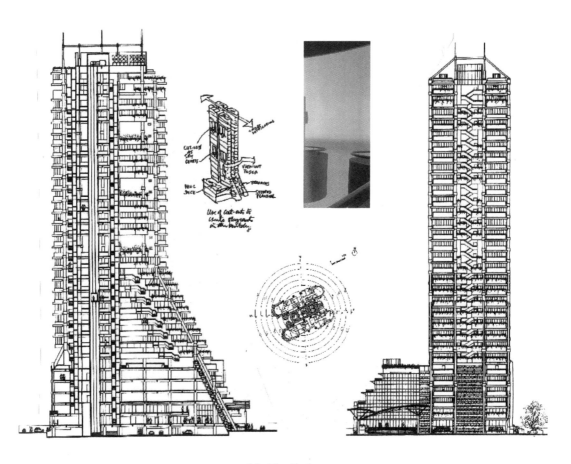

Tropical skyscrapers

Yeang's first high-rise design for IBM Plaza in Kuala Lumpur (1983) had the bold initiative to have greenery growing up the façade of the tower in a series of stepped planting boxes and then connecting with another series of planting boxes on the opposite side of the building with a mid-level planted court. It was the precursor of later ideas on green walls, biodiversity and ecological connectivity. The orientation of the tower relates to the specific sun path and wind rose of the location and building cores are placed on the hot east and west façades. In the design of another Kuala Lumpur tower – Plaza Atrium (1985) – Yeang placed the ubiquitous internal atrium associated with towers in temperate zones, on the outside of the building so that it could be naturally ventilated, planting could be introduced on balconies and louvres used at the roof level to filter sun and rain. The external atrium cre-

ates a wind shaft to cool the offices facing the atrium. And the 31-storey Menara Boustead, also in Kuala Lumpur and completed in 1986, had a number of additional innovative features. It has landscaped balconies encircling the circular tower block, with trickle irrigation ensuring a splendid growth of bougainvillea. The service core is located on the hot side of the building and is naturally ventilated thereby reducing the air-conditioning load on the offices.

In 1989 the first monograph of his work *Rethinking the Environmental Filter* recorded Yeang's early high-rise building in the tropics and anticipated further development of the Tropical skyscraper. But it was not until 1992 that Yeang completed another tower that attracted international attention. The 24-storey circular Menara Mesiniaga at Subang Jaya, Malaysia develops the idea of a spiralling green garden connected to the surrounding landscape and of sky courts and sky gardens culminating in a roof-

top swimming pool. Louvred panels protect the façades of the tower from solar gain and their design is determined by their orientation. Completed a year later, in 1993 the 31-storey Mbf Tower in Penang, is notable for its transitional spaces, two-storey sky courts and natural ventilation. Another tower, the 11-storey semi-circular Metrolux – Casa del Sol (1994) in Kuala Lumpur, features planted and terraced skycourts in a diagonal configuration stepping upwards from the centre. Naturally ventilated single-loaded corridors face the hot western side of the site and act as a buffer, reducing insolation. The apartments, the lift lobbies and the staircases are naturally ventilated. Completed two years later the 29-storey Central Plaza Tower (1996) has sunshading provided by deeply recessed balconies on the east elevation and planter boxes ascend diagonally up the north face of the building terminating at a poolside terrace.

Another seminal design by Yeang, the 21-storey Menara Umno (1998) in Penang, is orientated such that all the services are located on the southeast elevation thus protecting the tower from solar heat gain while the opposite elevation faces northwest and is clear glazed with deeply recessed windows and protective louvres. A unique feature of this tower is the "wind wing-wall" – a 21-storey high vertical projecting wall directed towards the prevailing wind. The wing-wall and its counterpart on the opposite elevation create positive and negative pressure zones and are remarkably effective in providing natural ventilation through common areas.

Bioclimatic skyscrapers

By the mid-1990s Yeang realised that the term "Tropical skyscraper" was too restrictive and the terminology had to become more generic. Consequently his focus shifted and *The Bioclimatic Skyscraper* published in 1994 signalled this realignment. Another book *Designing with Nature* (1995) emerged that was an edited and updated version of his PhD thesis and affirmed his ecological credentials. Yet another book, *The Skyscraper Bioclimatically Considered: A Design Primer* (1997) confirmed this shift of focus as did another book *The Green Skyscraper: The basis for designing sustainable intensive buildings* (1999).

As the end of the millennium approached the 26-storey EDITT Tower (1998) was designed for an urban site in Singapore. The physical compartmentation of floors that is inherent in the skyscraper typology inhibits continuity so Yeang's innovative proposal examined the idea of spatial continuity between street level and the tower. In creating vertical "places in the sky" the EDITT Tower sought to create a continuous spatial flow from the public realm to the private realm as a vertical extension of the street, eliminating the inherent stratification. The promoters of the competition did not build the EDITT Tower but the idea of the continuous landscaped ramp would be refined in later designs. Competitions (even unsuccessful ones) are a vehicle for exploring ideas that subsequently find their way into built projects.

Published in 1999, *Ken Yeang: Rethinking the Skyscraper* by Robert Powell recorded all Yeang's work until 1998 and shortly afterwards *The Ecology of the Sky* recorded a further shift in Yeang's "brand", towards an explicitly bioclimatic driven agenda. Powell's book identified aspects of urban design in Yeang's towers, a theme that would be explored by Yeang in a 2002 publication on a vertical theory of urban design, *Reinventing the Skyscraper: A Vertical Theory of Urban Design*.

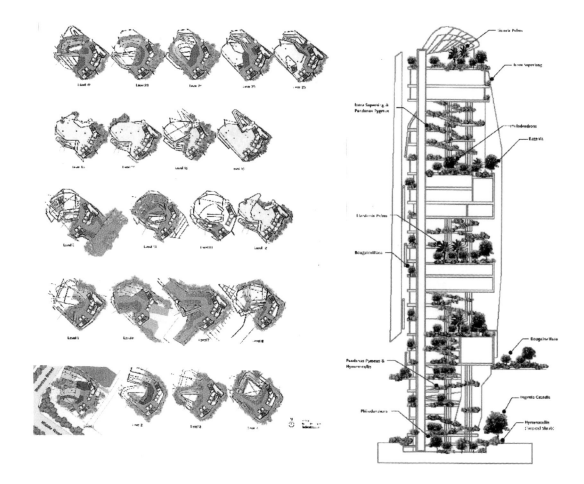

The Bishopsgate Tower (1999) was Yeang's first foray into the European market. The project in London included two 65-storey residential skyscrapers and one 50-storey office and hotel associated with a convention centre. This was an opportunity for Yeang to test his theoretical propositions on the green skyscrapers in a temperate climate and to outline the benefits of intensified vertical urban living. The residential blocks essentially have a radial plan-form with apartments forming a fan on the north and south façades. The peripheral apartments enclose an internal atrium that rises through the core of the tower encircled by a continuous landscaped ramp. The landscaped atrium is augmented by planted sky courts. Yeang introduces horizontal and vertical zoning in the form of a vertical masterplan with a public park at the 23rd floor. Similar in many ways to the EDITT Tower, the Bishopgate Tower utilises the same principles but they are modified for a northern European climate. Buildings are orientated to maximise solar gain into interior spaces in winter and to maximise solar shading in the summer months. Urban connectivity is a key ingredient in the design that utilises earth mounding and concrete eco-bridges.

Alongside a railway station the three residential towers at Elephant and Castle, London (2000), between 12 and 35 storeys high are located above a retail and commercial podium. The plates are oval and the elevator and staircase cores are located at the centre of each tower encircled by a ventilated and landscaped ramp. A number of landscaped sky-courts are inserted into the towers, and the apartments are orientated to achieve maximum solar exposure for passive heating in winter.

Globalising practice –
ecologically-driven design

In a decisive move to reach a global market for his ideas on ecologically driven design, in 2005 Yeang became Design Director of the UK-based practice of Llewelyn

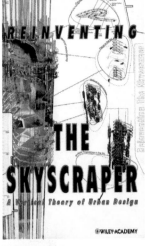

Davies. The skills of the two firms complimented each other and gave Yeang a base in the Northern Hemisphere.

Nevertheless the most progressive developments in eco skyscrapers are in Asia. The 16-storey high-rise National Library of Singapore (2005) consists of two interlinked blocks separated by a naturally-lit, semi-enclosed internal "street" with a louvred roof canopy. The library is designed as a low-energy, environment-responsive structure with a number of passive mode design strategies. The central atrium space, open at the base, creates a cool microclimate while allowing natural daylight to reach the circulation areas within the building. Wide sunshades control direct sunlight and glare besides creating the aesthetic of a contemporary climate-responsive built-form. The elevator cores serve as thermal buffers on the hot south-east façade, reducing solar heat gain. Green sky courts provide a relaxing environment for the library users while enhancing the site's biodiversity.

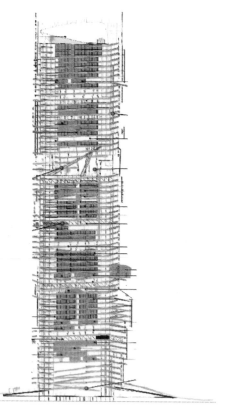

Views Analysis

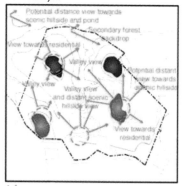

◌ View extents
■ Vantage Point above 80m
■ Vantage Point above 70m

Existing Vegetation

▨ Existing Land Clearing
▨ Oil Palm Grid

Solar Path & Wind Direction

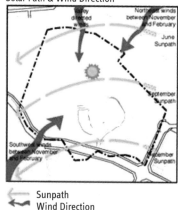

◀ Sunpath
◀ Wind Direction

Natural Drainage

◆ Ponds/lakes
🐾 Existing boundary abulting earthworks adge
◀■■ Major drainage/gulley channels
◀■ Slope drainage run off

The following year Yeang designed the Ecobay Complex in Abu Dhabi consisting of two residential towers, two office towers and one hotel rising out of a six-storey podium. The complex is conceptually a network of passively cooled vertical atria gardens and public spaces. Also in 2006 Yeang completed The Residence – TTDI Phase 6D1, a 21-storey residential block in Kuala Lumpur. It incorporates internal airwells combined with a wind scoop at the base of the tower to improve internal comfort. CFD analysis was carried out to understand sunlight penetration, solar gain and the sun-shades are based on a sun path study. Passive mode strategies result in a low energy consumption building.

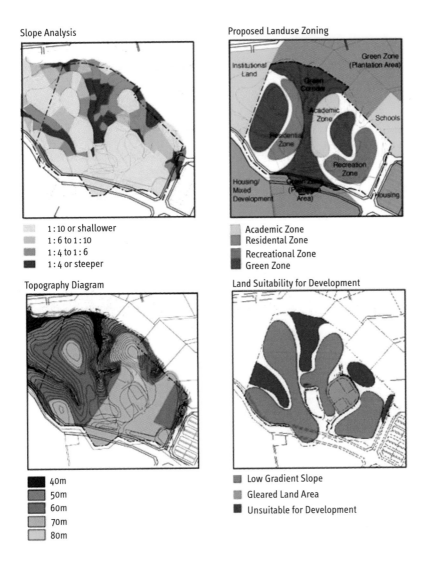

Slope Analysis

1 : 10 or shallower
1 : 6 to 1 : 10
1 : 4 to 1 : 6
1 : 4 or steeper

Proposed Landuse Zoning

Green Zone
(Plantation Area)

Institutional
Land

Green
Corridor

Academic
Zone

Schools

Residental
Zone

Recreation
Zone

Housing/
Mixed
Development

Green Zone
(Plantation
Area)

Housing

Academic Zone
Residental Zone
Recreational Zone
Green Zone

Topography Diagram

40m
50m
60m
70m
80m

Land Suitability for Development

Low Gradient Slope
Gleared Land Area
Unsuitable for Development

In the course of the next two years Yeang published two books developing the idea of the eco skyscraper namely *EcoDesign: A Manual for Ecological Design* (2006) and *Eco Skyscrapers* (2008). Other towers followed including Premier City in Almaty, Kazakhstan (2007) and Plaza of Nations in Vancouver, Canada (2008).

Spire Edge, currently under construction, will be India's first eco skyscraper located in the IT Millennium Park in Manesar. The key design feature is a continuous vegetated ramp moving up the south façade from the horizontal to the vertical plane. On the north façade, the landscape is brought up from the surrounding park with the

"peeling open" of the curtain wall to insert a series of sky courts. Two eco-cells are located on the north and south sides of the building and penetrate to the basement bringing in daylight, vegetation and natural ventilation. The project's climate-responsive façades originated from analysis of the sun path in Manesar. This determined the shape and depth of the sun louvres, which also act as light shelves to illuminate the office interiors. The single louvres on the north façade split into double louvres as they turn to the south to protect the curtain wall glazing from direct solar gain. The 21-storey tower integrates water catchment, retention, storage and recycling.

Zorlu (2008) was an invited competition for mixed-use development on a 9.6ha site overlooking the Bosphorus in Istanbul. There are 14 towers above a three-storey shopping and entertainment plinth with five floors of underground parking. A careful study was carried out of the sun path and wind characteristics in addition to

topography and hydrology. The KZBF and EIA Towers in
Abu Dhabi (2009) was another invited competition. The
brief required two 29-storey commercial towers, two
29-storey residential towers and a two-storey retail mall
above a basement car park on a site bordering mangrove
swamp. The design with four oval towers promotes ecological connectivity with an eco undercroft linking the
site to the mangrove. The towers incorporate ascending
green gardens from the podium level to the roofs and
high-rise landscaped bridges link the towers.

Another project in 2009 the 60-storey Jabi Lake Gardens
Hotel tower block in Nigeria is a direct response to the

local climate and seeks to create ecological connectivity with the surrounding area. Two cranked linear "wings" are arranged on a northeast/southwest axis joined by a central core comprising vertical circulation and sky courts. The linear blocks capture the prevailing winds and the orientation mitigates against the morning and evening heat gain when the sun is at low altitude. The hotel has a number of green features: sky courts, sky gardens and roof gardens,while "green walls" ascend the central core. Louvred screens and pergolas provide shade and prevent excessive solar gain. The sky gardens and sky courts permit hotel guests and owners of private apartments to enjoy the "in-between" space that are the hallmark of all successful buildings in the tropics. The hotel design aims to be "green" beyond all current measurement systems. Getting the basics right; such as correct orientation in relation to the sun path and the relationship to wind blowing over water go a long way towards producing an eco-friendly hotel.

The GyeongGi Provincial Government Office, Korea (2010) is a 46-storey tower that explicitly seeks to bring nature close to humans in the working environment with a High-Tech Vertical Forest. Approximately 4ha of green walls, green terraces and green roofs are incorporated in the tower, rising out of a landscaped podium and these employ native species to encourage biodiversity. The mapping of biodiversity is an important part of the design process. The design employs ground source heating and cooling. The unique climate responsive façade design has louvres that close in winter and open in summer.

Towards the end of 2010 Yeang, with Lillian Woo, published a Dictionary of Ecodesign and on the One-North site in Singapore masterplanned by Zaha Hadid Architects, TRHY completed a state of the art eco-tower – Solaris@Fusionopolis, a 15-storey + roofgarden, multi-tenanted media, science and engineering research centre. The tower exemplifies the plethora of possibilities inherent in an ecological approach to architecture.

The curved form of the Solaris building consists of two blocks connected by a naturally ventilated central atrium. Office floors are linked by a series of sky-bridges that span the atrium at the upper floors. The building's

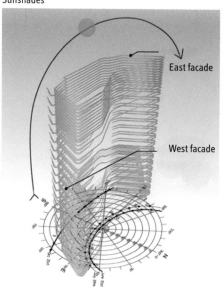

Sunshades

East facade

West facade

overall energy consumption is planned to show a reduction of 33% compared to local precedents.

Solaris has a 1.5 km continuous spiral landscaped ramp climbing the external wall and connecting at the base to the adjacent One-North Park. The ramp has over 8,000 square metres of vegetated area integrated into the built fabric that represents 113% of the project site area. The vegetated ramp can be considered as an urban eco-system. At the northeast corner of the building where the spiral ramp meets the ground is an "ecocell" that penetrates to the lowest level of the underground car park bringing daylight, vegetation and natural ventilation. Rainwater is harvested and stored in tanks at the base of the ecocell and thereafter it is pumped to the upper levels for irrigation purposes. The continuity of the landscaping on the ramp is a key component of the ecological strategy as it permits the movement of plant and in-

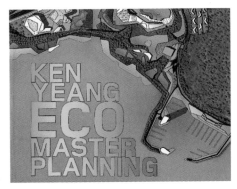

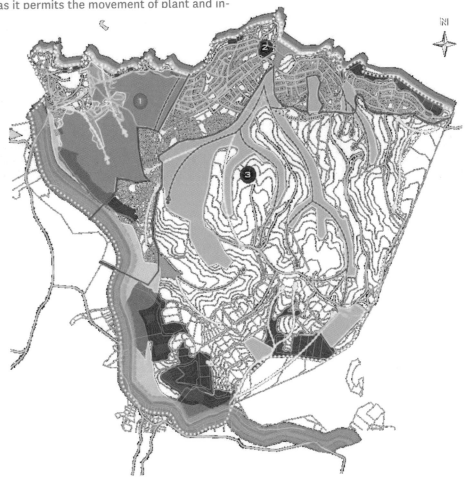

sect species that enhances biodiversity. The landscape helps to balance the inherent inorganic qualities of the built form. The vertical landscape is intended to act as a thermal buffer. The ramp allows for interaction between office occupants and nature.

Façade studies analysing the solar path determined the shape and depth of the sunshade louvres which also serve as light shelves, bouncing light into the building. The solar shading strategy reduces heat transfer to the building's low-E double-glazed perimeter façade contributing to an extremely low external thermal transfer value (ETTV) of 39 watts per square metre. The sunshade louvres contribute to achieving a comfortable microclimate in the working spaces that abut the building exterior. A diagonal shaft slices through the upper floors of Tower A allowing daylight to penetrate to the building's interior. Internal lighting operates on a system of sensors that reduce energy use by automatically turning off lights when adequate daylight is available.

The public plaza between the two tower blocks is a naturally ventilated space that operates as mixed-mode zone (Non-airconditioned) with an operable glass louvred roof over the atrium providing protection from the elements while permitting full ventilation when required. Computational fluid dynamic (CFD) simulations were used to analyse thermal conditions and wind speed within the atrium. The results were used to optimise the atrium façade design to improve airflow and enhance comfort levels.

At the time of writing LDY are working on yet another skyscraper – the 42-storey Bombay Glassworks Tower in Mumbai where we are attempting once again to push forward the frontiers of eco design as every apartment is given a sky-garden with access at every fifth level to a landscaped communal sky-court.

The Eco skyscraper

One of the major challenges in an architectural practice is how to develop a continuous programme of research given the cyclical nature of the economy and the disparate requirements of individual clients. TRHY and LDY resolutely pursue Yeang's agenda to create Ecoskyscrapers in a continuously evolving and iterative research programme.

About the Authors

Han Meyer

Han (V.J.) Meyer is Professor of Theory and Methods of Urban Design at Delft University of Technology. His research concerns the transformations of port cities, the fundamentals of the discipline of urbanism, the development of the Dutch urban block, the present state-of-the-art of Dutch urbanism, and "Delta-urbanism".

Peter Bosselmann

Peter Bosselmann has taught urban design at the University of California, Berkeley since 1984 and held endowed chairs at Tokyo University, Royal Danish Academy of Art in Copenhagen, Milan Polytechnico, and South China University of Technology in Guangzhou. He works internationally on urban design and planning projects. He is currently completing a publication on the metropolitan landscape, and his previous books include *Urban Transformation – Understanding City Design and Form* by Island Press, 2008 and *Representation of Places: Reality and Realism in City Design,* UC Press, 1998. Together with his students he maintains a Global Metropolitan Observatory at www.ced.Berkeley.edu/research/metropolitanlandscapes

Markus Appenzeller

Markus Appenzeller is Principal at MLA+, a practice that works on complex urban and architectural topics worldwide. He is a studio professor at the Berlage Institute in Rotterdam/Delft and lectures regularly on contemporary urban questions. His research focuses on the future of the mid-size European city, and on urban regeneration, particularly in fast-growing agglomerations.

Lora Nicolaou

Lora Nicolaou is Principal at LMN Design, and Visiting Professor at Frederick University, Cyprus. She is an architect, with postgraduate studies in Urban Design in London and Oxford, where she taught Urban Design for many years. She was the Director of Urban Strategies at DEGW from 1997–2009, and held a parallel post as the Head of Research for the Urban Renaissance Institute (URI) at the University of Greenwich from 2004–10. She has now established her own design consultancy firm (LMN) practicing across architecture, strategic briefing, masterplanning and planning research on projects across Europe. In addition she is Visiting Professor at Frederick University, School of Architecture, Cyprus. Her recent work includes "city" and "tall building" strategies for Dublin, Rotterdam, London, Cambridge, Utrecht, Hereford, Gothenburg and Nicosia. She has an extensive portfolio of publications on aspects of urban morphology and workplace briefing.

Daan Zandbelt

Daan Zandbelt graduated from Delft University of Technology as an architect and urban designer, and studied at the University of Illinois at Chicago. In 2002 he founded Zandbelt&vandenBerg, architecture and urban design, in Rotterdam with Rogier van den Berg. Since 2003 he has been part of the Chair of Metropolitan and Regional Design at Delft University of Technology, where he is currently assistant professor. At Zandbelt&vandenBerg he is responsible for architecture and urbanism projects as diverse as a Villa in the Dunes to long-term development plans for the Amsterdam-Schiphol region. He also frequently publishes articles and books on urban issues.

Meta Berghauser Pont

Meta Berghauser Pont is a researcher working at the Department of Urbanism of Delft University of Technology and at the Royal Institute of Technology (KTH) in Stockholm, Sweden. She defended her PhD thesis in 2009 in which she, together with Per Haupt, developed a method to measure density so that it can be related in a meaningful way to urban form and other performances. This work was published by NAi Publishers in 2010 as *Spacematrix. Space, Density and Urban Form.* Since its publication, this performative approach to urban form has been further developed in cooperation with other researchers.

Emiel Arends

Emiel Arends (1977) studied Planning at the Rijkshogeschool IJsselland, Deventer, and Urban Planning at the Rotterdam Academy of Architecture and Urban Design. Since 2001, he has been working for the city of Rotterdam as an urban designer, where he has contributed to a variety of projects and masterplans, including the *Kop van Zuid*, *Parkstad*, and the *Central Station Quarter*; he has also been involved in strategies for the inner city, including high-rise and sustainability. Emiel is a guest lecturer at Delft University of Technology and writes articles for national and international journals.

Frank van der Hoeven

Frank van der Hoeven is Associate Professor of Urban Design at the Faculty of Architecture at Delft University of Technology. He conducted his PhD research in the field of underground space technology and multifunctional and intensive land-use. The core of his work deals with urban design issues related to mixed-use development: transit-oriented development, urban greenhouse horticulture, the use of underground space, high-rise urban areas, and recently climate change. Currently he combines his associate professorship in Urban Design with the position of Research Director of the Faculty of Architecture at TU Delft.

Steffen Nijhuis

Steffen Nijhuis is Assistant Professor of Landscape Architecture at the Department of Urbanism at Delft University of Technology. His PhD research, entitled *Mapping landscape architectonic compositions with GIS,* focuses on the application of Geographic Information Science in landscape architecture research and design. The core of his work deals with theories, methods and techniques in the field of landscape architecture and urban design: design research, research by design, visual landscape assessment, and visual knowledge representation. He leads the research program Architecture and Landscape, is series editor of RiUS, and advises governmental and regional authorities in the Netherlands.

Andy van den Dobbelsteen

Andy van den Dobbelsteen is a Full Professor of Climate Design & Sustainability at the Faculty of Architecture of Delft University of Technology. He lectures and leads research projects in various areas of sustainability in the built environment. Andy has written numerous publications, both scientific and popular. He has chaired various conferences, among them the award-winning *SASBE 2009, Nationale Dubo Dag,* and *Nationaal Congres Energie & Ruimte.* Andy is joint coordinator of the CIB Working Commission 116. Andy was external examiner at the Manchester School of Architecture and a visiting fellow at the Melbourne Sustainable Society Institute.

Kees Kaan

Kees Kaan graduated in architecture at Delft University of Technology in 1987. A founding partner of Claus en Kaan Architecten, he has built up an international range of projects; he has recently won competitions for the masterplan El Prat de Llobregat in Barcelona, a building for Chambre des Métiers et de l'Artisanat in Lille, the Pharmacy building on the campus of the University of Granada, and the Royal Museum of Fine Arts in Antwerp. Realized projects include the Crematorium Heimolen in Sint-Niklaas, Belgium, the Netherlands Forensic Institute in The Hague, and the Royal Netherlands Embassy in Maputo, Mozambique. He is currently the supervisor of the Lijnbaan district in Rotterdam and the Technopolis Science Park in Delft, and has been a juror for many international architectural competitions. Since 2006, he has held the chair in Materialization as a Professor of Architectural Design at the Delft University of Technology.

Robert Powell

Robert Powell was Associate Professor of Architecture at the National University of Singapore (1984–2001). He is currently Project Director and Head of Ecomasterplanning with Llewelyn Davies Yeang (UK). He is the author of 30 books including *Ken Yeang: Rethinking the Environmental Filter* (1989) and *Ken Yeang: Rethinking the Skyscraper* (1999).

High-rise and the
Sustainable City